EASY TO MAKE

NEW CHRISTMAS CRAFTS

EASY TO MAKE

NEW CHRISTMAS CRAFTS

Kerrie Dudley

ANAYA PUBLISHERS LTD LONDON

First published in Great Britain in 1993 by
Anaya Publishers Ltd, Strode House,
44–50 Osnaburgh Street, London NW1 3ND

Editor: Eve Harlow
Designed by: Design 23
Photography: Steve Tanner
Cover photography: Shona Wood
Illustrator: Kate Simunek

British Library Cataloguing in Publication data

Dudley, Kerrie
Easy to make: New Christmas Crafts – (Easy to make)
I. Title II. Series
ISBN 1 85470 157 6

Typeset by Servis Filmsetting Ltd, Manchester, UK
Colour reproduction by Scantrans Pte Ltd, Singapore
Printed and bound in Hong Kong

CONTENTS

Introduction   6

1: WELCOME TO CHRISTMAS
Advent calendar   10
King card holder   14
Rope of flowers   18
Three ships   20
Flower cones   23
Christmas scene   24

2: THE NIGHT BEFORE CHRISTMAS
Gift stockings for the family   30
Wooden toys   32
Beanbag toys   35
Santa puppet   38
Reindeer mascot   41

3: SPECIALLY FOR THE TREE
Glittering decos   46
Golden bells   48
Lacy fairy   50
Christmas folk   53
Baubles and bows   55
Not-so-heavenly choir   57
Musical tree trims   60
Soft hearts   62
Christmas geese   64

4: SET THE TABLE
Buffet table decoration   68
Lacy tree   70
Reindeer holiday cloth   72
Happy snowman   75
Appliqué candle   78
Pleated paper tree   80

5: CHRISTMAS WORKSHOP
Great little character toys   84
Christmas robin picture   87
Desert scene greeting card   89
Cross stitched greeting cards   92
Gift cans   94

BETTER TECHNIQUES
Useful addresses and acknowledgements   112

Introduction

In the olden days, most Christmas gifts and decorations were lovingly made by hand. Now, with the help of this book, some of the magic of an old-fashioned Christmas can be recaptured.

Christmas is a happy holiday in many countries throughout the world and, for the Christian church, celebrates what many consider to be its most important event, the birth of Jesus Christ. Different countries have different customs and traditions and, in most, Christmas is a combination of religious and pagan festivals which have become intermingled over hundreds of years. But whether you call Father Christmas Santa Claus, Saint Nicholas or Kriss Kringle, he is still a jolly old man as full of generosity and goodwill as the spirit of Christmas itself.

Christmas is the season to bring joy to others, for homecomings and family reunions, for feasting, festivity and fun. And, for this most colourful and joyous season, we transform our homes with evergreens, trees and glittering decorations, and give presents to our families and friends. In the chapter called 'Welcome to Christmas' you will find a wealth of ideas for hand-made decorations to give your home a character all of its own, and which are not only fun to make, but will also help keep costs down. In 'Christmas Workshop' you will find ideas for gifts which will be treasured far more than any shop-bought present.

In this electronic age, it is good to retain some of the old skills, whether they are traditional crafts such as woodcarving, candlemaking or flower arranging or one of the relatively new ones like embroidery on plastic canvas, foilcraft or appliqué using no-sew techniques. You will find both old and new crafts in these pages.

A variety of crafts for people of all ages and levels of skill is also to be found here. Even if you have never picked up a needle before, you will be able to make shiny fabric bells, or embroider jolly toy characters to hang on your tree. For the more experienced at needlecrafts there is a cheerful robin picture to work in crewel embroidery. The papercrafts include simple but stunning tree decorations made from old sheet music and a pretty table-top tree made from Christmas giftwrap and some unusual cards to make your greetings more personal.

Making something from nothing can be very satisfying because we know we are helping to conserve the world's resources by recycling waste and saving money at the same time. Some of the projects are ideal for children and include nativity figures based on plastic bottles, tree decorations made from plastic bags, cardboard tubes transformed into amusing characters and throw-away cans turned into attractive containers.

Children's Christmas
The time leading up to Christmas is all a part of the fun. For most children, Christmas starts when the shops and streets are decorated and the lights go on,

but the big day still seems a long way off. The robin advent calendar will help with their continuous question of 'How many days?' before they can hang their stockings. Depending on their age, of course, children might be able to help in the making of the calendar by painting the robins and cutting out the beaks and tails.

The chapter 'The Night before Christmas' includes stockings for all the family and a few ideas for toys which you could make to help Santa out. These stocking fillers will help keep the children occupied during the early hours of Christmas morning!

Decorating the tree

Christmas would not be complete without the tree. Many homes now decorate an outside tree with lights and the one indoors is often positioned in front of a window so that passers by can share the beauty. As a child I remember walking my grandmother home on Christmas night, counting the trees in the windows and enjoying the cosy scenes inside. I am sure that for children today, decorating the tree is one of the highlights of the festive season, just as it has always been.

In the 'Specially for the tree' chapter there are lots of fun ideas including choirboys made from paper and table tennis balls, geese made from towelling socks and a cheerful fairy for the top.

Not all countries are lucky enough (or unlucky enough, depending on your age!) to have snow at this festive time, but everyone seems to dream about a white Christmas, so you will love the debonair snowman table centre made from papier mâché. The body is hollow and can be filled with small gifts for the family.

There are many other decorations to add sparkle to your festive table and adorn your home, and whatever your traditions, I hope you find something to make from this book which will help bring back the magic of Christmas you knew as a child and to make this holiday one that your chidren will remember all through their lives.

SAFETY NOTES

Most of the projects in this book are decorations rather than toys and should be kept out of the reach of young children. When making the stocking fillers, observe the safety suggestions in the instructions and ensure that all features and accessories are sewn on securely.

When using adhesives, paints, sprays etc, follow the directions on the container. Protect your work surfaces and when you are using craft knives keep your fingers clear of the cutting edge. Always supervise children, especially where cutting is involved.

Decorations are usually inflammable so make sure they are displayed safely and, in particular, not too close to an open fire. Never leave a naked flame – such as a lighted candle – unattended and always replace it before it burns too low.

ONE

Welcome to Christmas

Advent calendar

Twenty-four robins all eagerly awaiting the big day. This advent calendar is as good as a Christmas tree, and with a tiny gift in each stocking it is sure to be very popular with children.

Materials
24 table tennis balls
48 black pipe-cleaners
Felt squares in assorted colours
Ribbon, ¼in (6mm) wide
Fusible web
7yds (7m) plastic-coated garden wire
Small pieces of stiff paper, black, orange and white
Red, white and brown acrylic paints
Glitter fabric pen
Gold thread
Thick florists' wire; binding wire
3 pieces of tinsel 60in (1.5m) long
Sheet of gold card
Ribbon for a bow
All-purpose glue
Contact adhesive (or a glue gun)

Preparation
1 Pierce two holes in each table tennis ball, approximately ¾in (18mm) apart, for inserting the robin's legs later.

2 Trim the fluff from the pipe-cleaners to make them thinner.

3 Trace the stocking pattern onto tracing (or grease-proof) paper. Using the pattern, cut out 48 stockings from felt, allowing ½in (12mm) extra all round for seams.

4 Cut ribbon strips the width of the stocking tops. Iron strips of fusible web to the back. Peel off the paper backing and iron the ribbon strips onto each of the stocking pieces.

5 Use wire cutters to cut lengths of garden wire as follows: 3 pieces 32in (81cm) long (A); 2 pieces 28in (71cm) long (B); 2 pieces 24in (60cm) long (C); 2 pieces 20in (50cm) long (D).

Working the design
6 Bend each of the pipe-cleaners into legs and claws. Coat the top 1½in (4cm) with glue and insert the legs into the holes in the table tennis balls. Allow to dry.

7 Trace the tail shape and cut 24 from white paper. Stick the tails in place with glue. Paint the robins (see the picture).

8 Trace the beak shape. Cut 24 from orange paper and fold in half. Cut 48 eyes from black paper. Stick the eyes and beaks in place. Paint a white highlight on each eye.

9 Pin or baste 2 stocking pieces together, right sides out. Stitch around the stockings. Trim the edges close to the stitching. Draw numbers from 1–24 on both sides using the glitter fabric pen and allow to dry. Sew gold thread through the top of each stocking to make a hanging loop.

10 **Tree:** Use thick florists' wire to bind the three A pieces of garden wire together 4in (10cm) from one end. Bend the two outer wires to form the top two branches. Then bind the two B wires to the stem 6½in (16.5cm) below and bend these to form branches. Repeat with the C and D wires, each 6½in (16.5cm) below. Bend to make the branches. Finally, bend back the end of each branch ½in (1cm) so that there are no sharp ends. Bend the top of the tree into a small loop. Thread a piece of ribbon through the loop to hang the tree on the wall.

11 Wind tinsel around the branches and the trunk, securing it in place with binding wire.

12 Gold pot: Using a protractor and ruler, draw the pot pattern on the wrong side of the gold card. Score and fold on the broken lines. Bend the front section into half a pot shape and stick the tab at the back. Cut a piece of gold card to fit in the top of the pot and cut a cross in this to push the tree trunk through. Stick the card into the pot. Stick the trunk into the pot using contact glue.

13 Hang the stockings on the branches. Position the robins and use pliers to wrap the feet around the branches. Secure the feet with a dot of contact glue or wire them on with binding wire.

14 Make a bow for the pot and stick in place. Cut a card star for the top of the tree.

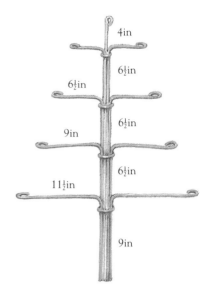

Bend the wire tree like this to make branches.

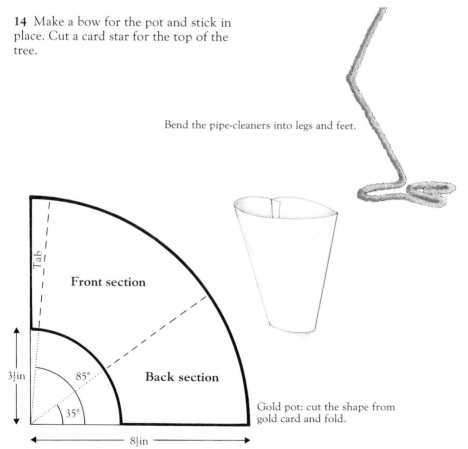

Bend the pipe-cleaners into legs and feet.

Gold pot: cut the shape from gold card and fold.

Trace this stocking and robin's detail pieces

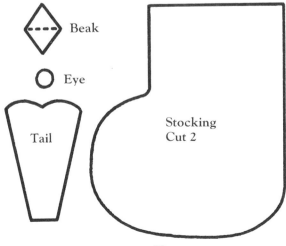

Beak

Eye

Tail

Stocking
Cut 2

King card holder

The card holder stands about 36in (90cm) high and will hold up to 28 cards. Make three kings to stand in your hallway or you could adapt the design to make smaller ones for a table decoration.

Materials

6 sheets of 20 × 30in (50 × 75cm) red card
2 sheets of 20 × 30in (50 × 75cm) white card
1 sheet of 20 × 30in (50 × 75cm) gold card
6yd (6m) approximately of gold paper lace cake trim
Brown, black and white cartridge paper
Squared pattern paper
Plastic 'jewels' with flat backs; a small piece of coloured foil
2yd (2m) approximately of $\frac{1}{4}$in (6mm)-wide gold ribbon or braid
Clear sticky tape
All-purpose glue; latex adhesive

Preparation

1 The red and white cards are used for the base. To make each base segment, score a line down the middle of the sheets of card (AB). Fold along this line. Mark a point (C) on the edge, 6in (15cm) up from the bottom left-hand corner. Draw a line joining C to A. Draw a line joining C to B. Cut along these lines (AC and BC) through both thicknesses. (Any card left over can be used to make small kings or Christmas cards.)

2 Cut 2in (5cm) slits in the folded edges of the segments at right angles to the base (AC) to take the cards. The slits should be about 6in (15cm) apart.

3 Stick pieces of cake trim about 1in (2.5cm) from the bottom edge of the segment (AC).

Working the design

4 Open out the segments and join them together on the wrong side of the long edges with sticky tape.

5 Head: Draw the head pattern to size. Trace the shape onto the back of the gold card. Cut out and form into an open-ended cone overlapping and gluing the join at the back. Cut the face area from the pattern and cut from brown paper. Stick in place on the gold cone, overlapping the join at the back.

6 Draw the beard pattern on squared paper. Cut out and then cut the beard from black paper. Curl each strand by winding it tightly around a knitting needle. Stick the beard to the face.

7 Trace the nose and eye patterns. Cut the nose in brown paper, fold along the broken lines. Fold the side tabs and stick the nose to the face.

8 Cut two eyes from white and black paper and stick in place. Draw a black line along the top of the eyes with a felt tip pen. Cut a curved strip of black paper for the mouth and stick in place. (Or, if you prefer, draw the mouth with a thick black pen.)

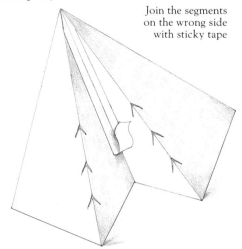

Join the segments on the wrong side with sticky tape

9 Crown: Cut a 2½in (6cm)-diameter circle of foil. Stick to the centre front of the crown. Stick on the plastic 'jewels'. Stick gold ribbon around the top and bottom edges of the golden crown.

10 The head rests on the body for display. When the card holder is completed, it will stand on its base quite safely. Slip greeting cards into the slits.

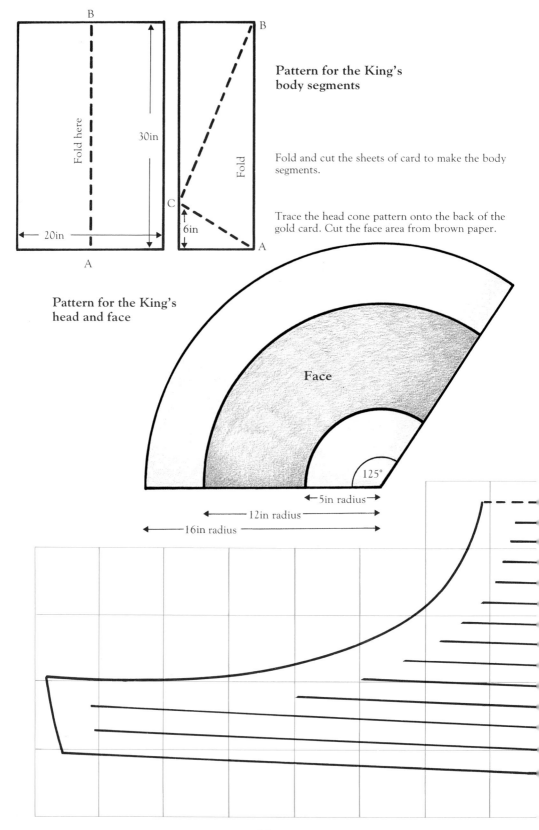

Pattern for the King's body segments

B

A

Fold here

20in

30in

B

Fold

C

6in

A

Pattern for the King's head and face

Fold and cut the sheets of card to make the body segments.

Trace the head cone pattern onto the back of the gold card. Cut the face area from brown paper.

Face

125°

5in radius

12in radius

16in radius

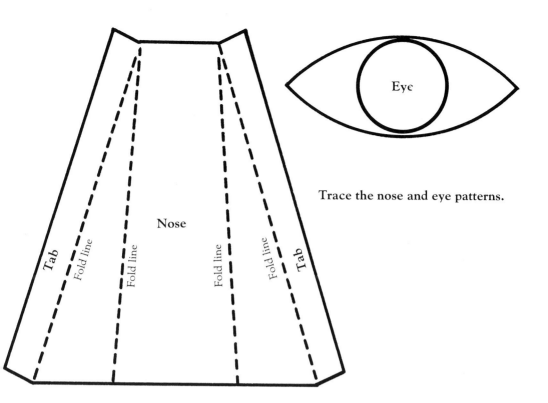

Nose

Tab

Fold line

Fold line

Fold line

Fold line

Tab

Eye

Trace the nose and eye patterns.

Beard: scale 1 sq = $\frac{1}{2}$in (1cm).

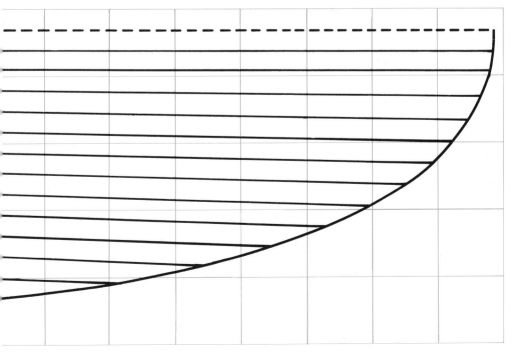

Rope of flowers

A flower rope decorated with dried flowers in Christmas colours makes a striking display. Hang one on either side of the fireplace, but take care not to have it too close to the fire.

Materials
34in (86.5cm) of thick plaited raffia rope
Four 1in (2.5cm) cubes of florists' dry
    foam
20 red, dried flower heads
Pieces of atracxa
8 dried poppy seed heads
Pieces of briza segromi
Silver and gold spray paint
1yd (90cm) of ribbon, 1in (2.5cm) wide
Florists' wire
All-purpose glue (or a glue gun)

Preparation
1 Stick the foam cubes onto the rope at even intervals. Spray the atracxa and 4 poppy heads gold.

2 Spray the briza segromi and the remaining poppy heads silver.

3 Wire the flower heads.

Working the design
4 Insert small pieces of the briza segromi around the bases of each of the foam cubes so that it extends over the rope.

5 Fill in the cubes with small pieces of atracxa so that no foam is visible.

6 Insert the poppy heads into the opposite corners of the foam cubes, alternating 2 gold heads and 2 silver heads.

7 Insert one flower into the centre and one on each face of all the cubes.

8 Make ribbon bows for the top and bottom of the rope and wire or stick them in place.

18

Flower napkin rings can be made in colour schemes to match your table centre. Cut a cardboard tube into 'slices' using a sharp crafts' knife. Bind the rings with white crêpe paper strips. Cut strips of coloured crêpe paper to fit round the rings with an extra ¼in (6mm) top and bottom to go over to the inside. Stick to the rings. Cut strips of crêpe paper to fit inside the rings. Stick dried flowers to small circles of cardboard. Leave to dry, then stick the circles to the napkin rings.

Three ships

These window decorations look like stained glass but they are made from card and acetate sheet covered with transparent film. Other simple shapes could be used.

Materials
Black cartridge paper
Card for a template
Thick acetate sheet
Coloured self-adhesive film
Double-sided tape
Clear sticky tape
Chinagraph pencil
Gold thread

Preparation
1 Trace the ship and make a template from card.

2 Cut two pieces of black paper approximately 1in (2.5cm) larger all round than the ship. Use sticky tape around the edges to stick these, one on top of the other, to a cutting surface.

3 Draw around the ship template on the top surface. Using a very sharp craft knife and cutting through both thicknesses, carefully cut away all the centre sections and finally around the outline. This will give you two black paper ships.

Working the design
4 Lay the ship tracing under the acetate sheet and draw around it using the chinagraph pencil.

5 Cut out the acetate approximately ⅛in (3mm) inside this line so that the acetate is slightly smaller than the black paper ships. Use small pieces of double-sided tape to fix the acetate to one of the ships.

6 Referring to the picture for the colours, lay the other paper ship on the paper backing of the selected self-adhesive film. (Because you will be drawing on the back of the self-adhesive film, the ship should be pointing in the opposite direction from the ship covered with acetate.)

7 Draw around the inside of the segment you wish to colour (for example one of the sails). Cut out each piece of self-adhesive film approximately ⅛in (3mm) larger than the drawn shape.

8 Peel off the paper backing and stick the piece carefully to the ship covered with acetate, squeezing out air bubbles as you go. To increase the colour range you can use two different colours, one on top of the other (for example the ship's hull is red on blue).

Cut out the acetate slightly smaller than the black paper ships. Use small pieces of double-sided tape to fix the acetate to one of the ships.

Trace this outline of the ship

9 When all the colours are in place use small pieces of double-sided tape to stick the two ships together making a sandwich of the now coloured acetate.

10 Use a needle to thread a length of gold thread through the acetate at the point of the small flag so that the ship is balanced when hanging.

Ships of gold and silver
For a different effect, try sticking pieces of two-sided foil between the cut-out paper ships. They will flash in currents of air.

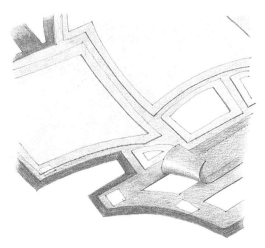

Stick the pieces of self-adhesive film over the coloured acetate.

Flower cones

Fir cones always look festive at Christmas, and this simple but attractive wall decoration could be used as an alternative to the traditional door wreath.

Materials
3 large fir cones
3 small rings of florists' dry foam
3yds (3m) approximately of 2½in (6cm)-
  wide ribbon
1½yds (1.5m) approximately of narrow
  red ribbon
Red achillea
Honesty
Sea lavender
Pieces of atracxa sprayed gold
Stem wire
All-purpose glue (or a glue gun)

Preparation
1 For each fir cone, position a 10in (25cm) piece of wire over the base, making a small loop (through which the ribbon can later be threaded) and wind the ends of the wire around the base so that they disappear between the seed husks.

2 Glue the foam ring onto the cone base.

Working the design
3 Fill the ring with sprigs of honesty and sea lavender until the foam is covered.

4 Insert the achillea and gold atracxa at evenly-spaced intervals (refer to the picture).

5 Cut the narrow ribbon into 3 uneven lengths. Tie the ribbon ends to the wire loops of the cones so that the cones hang at different levels (see picture).

6 Tie the top ends of ribbon together, slip a piece of wire through and twist the ends to make a hanging loop.

7 Make a large bow with the wide ribbon. Glue the bow over the ends of the narrow ribbons. If you prefer, use crushed paper ribbon for the bow. This comes in a twisted robe and, opened out, makes large, flamboyant bows.

Christmas scene

Each figure is about 9in (23cm) tall, so this nativity set is large enough to display in a school or church during Advent. It is quite cheap to make as it uses throw-away plastic bottles and paper.

Materials
1.5 litre plastic fizzy drink bottles
2¾in (7cm)-diameter foam, or cotton pulp, balls
Brown stockings or tights
Crêpe paper in assorted colours
Small amount of polyester toy filling
Black, brown and grey cartridge paper
16 pipe-cleaners (for arms)
6 orange pipe-cleaners
3 plastic 'jewels' for crowns
Gold card
Scraps of braid
3 beads or trinkets (gifts for kings)
1in (2.5cm) cotton pulp ball
Latex adhesive

Preparation
1 Using a craft knife cut off the tops of the bottles, leaving about ¼in (6mm) of the neck still protruding. Cut the bottom from the bottles 6in (15cm) down from the new top.

2 Make a groove in the bottom of each large ball by pushing it gently onto the neck of the bottle.

Working the design
3 Each head ball is covered with a 6in (15cm) tube of stocking or tights cut from the leg. First, tie the tube around the middle. Put the ball in one end of the tube with the groove at the end and fold the other half of the tube back over the ball so that it is covered with a double thickness. Gather the tube ends together and tie tightly with thread. (This part will fit into the neck.)

4 Cover the body by rolling it in a 9 × 12in (23 × 30cm) piece of crêpe paper

with the grain running crossways on the paper (this will be vertical on the figure). Stick the overlap with dots of adhesive at the back and tuck the excess crêpe paper at the top and bottom inside the bottle, sticking it in place.

5 Make belts for the shepherds, Mary and Joseph from 12 × 1½in (30 × 4cm) strips of crêpe paper with the grain running lengthways. Fold into thirds along the length and glue around the body.

6 Spread adhesive on the crêpe-covered bottle neck and push the head firmly onto it so that the neck fits into the groove in the ball. The excess stocking is hidden inside the bottle. Hold the head in place until the glue is quite dry.

Tie the stocking tube round the middle, put the head ball into one end.

7 Nose: Run a gathering thread round the edge of a 1in (2.5cm)-diameter circle of stocking. Pull up the gathers, stuff lightly with toy stuffing and tie off. Make a nose for each figure.

8 Cut eyes and beards from paper and stick the features in place.

9 Hands: Run a gathering thread round the edges of a 2in (5cm) diameter circle of stocking. Pull up the gathers, stuff with toy stuffing and tie off. Dip one end of a pipe-cleaner in adhesive and push it into the hand. Bend the other end of the pipe-cleaner so that the arm and hand together measures 4¼in (11cm) long. Make 2 hands for each figure.

10 Sleeves: Cut a 4in (10cm)-radius circle of paper. Fold in four, cut out one segment for a sleeve pattern. Cut 2 sleeves for each figure from crêpe paper with the grain running from the point to the centre of the curved edge. Lay an arm on a sleeve with the hand extending over the curved edge. Fold one edge of the sleeve over onto the arm, securing with dots of adhesive on the hand at the top of the arm. Bring over the other edge and glue on top of the first to make a loose sleeve. Repeat with the other arm, so that the glued seams are at the back.

11 Mary and Joseph's head-dresses:
Cut a 8 × 18in (20 × 45cm) piece of crêpe paper with the grain running lengthways. Fold under 1in (2.5cm) along one long side and place the middle of the folded edge to the middle of the forehead. Hold the middle of the opposite edge down at the back of the figure. Bring the two sides across and secure with dots of adhesive. Make a headband from a 1 × 10in (2.5 × 25cm) strip of crêpe paper with the grain running lengthways. Fold into thirds along the length and stick around the head, making small tucks in the front of the head-dress on each side.

12 Make a shepherd's head-dress in the same way with a 7 × 10in (18 × 25cm) piece of crêpe paper. Make the crooks from three pipe-cleaners. Cut one in half and glue each half to the end of a complete pipe-cleaner. Twist together and bend into a crook.

13 Kings: For a cape, cut a 6 × 20in (15 × 50cm) strip of crêpe paper with the grain running crossways. Run a gathering thread ½in (1cm) from one long edge. Pull up the gathers to fit around the neck and tie in place.

14 For the hair, cut a 5 × 8½in (12.5 × 21.5cm) strip of crêpe paper with the grain running crossways. Fold in half along the length. Cut out a section for the face. Stick the folded side around the head so that the bottom edge is just above the neck. Make small tucks at the top edge to fit the curve of the head.

15 To make a king's crown, cut a 2in (5cm)-wide strip of gold card and form into a circle to fit the head. Stick the overlap. Cut the edge decoratively. Gather the edge of a 4in (10cm)-diameter circle of crêpe paper for the inside of the crown. Push it into the crown from the bottom, pull up gathers to fit and stick in place. Stick the crown on the head and decorate with a 'jewel'.

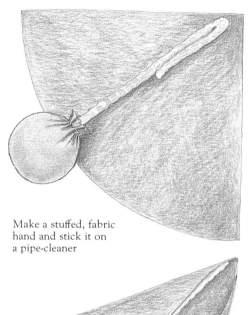

Make a stuffed, fabric hand and stick it on a pipe-cleaner

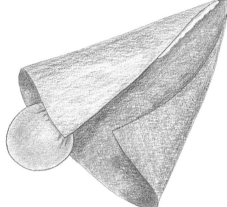

Fold one sleeve edge over the other and stick down.

16 Stick braid around the bottom of the kings' robes, and stick the gifts to the hands.

17 Baby: Twist two pipe-cleaners into arms, legs and body and stick the neck into the small cotton pulp ball. Cut a 2in (5cm)-diameter circle of double thickness stocking fabric. Run a gathering thread around the edges. Pull up gathers loosely, fit the head inside and tie tightly around the neck. For the shawl, cut a 6 × 9½in (15 × 24cm) piece of crêpe paper with the grain running lengthways. Fold under 1in (2.5cm) along one long side and glue the centre of this side to the baby's forehead. Fold the rest of the shawl around the baby and glue the baby to Mary's arms.

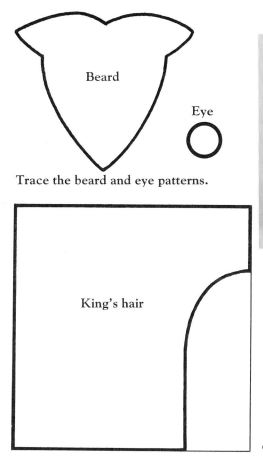

Beard

Eye

Trace the beard and eye patterns.

King's hair

Cut the crêpe paper for the kings' hair like this.

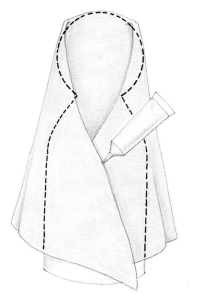

Bring the sides of the head-dress across at the back and secure with adhesive.

Twist 2 pipe-cleaners together to make the baby's body.

TWO

The night before Christmas

❧

Gift stockings for the family

These stockings are decorated using a no-sew appliqué technique. Simply iron on motifs cut from print fabric using fusible web to bond, then paint the outline with a fabric glitter pen.

Materials
(For three stockings)
Squared pattern paper
40in (1m) of 44in (112cm)-wide plain, quilted red and green fabric
12in (30cm) of 44in (112cm)-wide print fabric for each stocking
Fusible web
Glitter fabric painting pen
6in (15cm) piece of ribbon for each stocking

Preparation
1 Draw the pattern on squared pattern paper. Cut out. Pin the pattern to a double thickness of quilted fabric, with what is to be the main stocking colour on the right side. Cut the fabric off level ·with the top edge of the paper pattern. Cut out around the pattern allowing ½in (1cm) all round.

2 For each stocking, cut 1¾in (4.5cm)-wide strips of the print fabric on the bias to make bias binding. Join the ends to make a strip about 48in (122cm) long.

3 Iron fusible web on to the back of some of the remaining print fabric and cut out several motifs.

Working the design
4 To make the cuff, fold the top edge down 4in (10cm) and then fold the raw edge under ½in (1cm). Pin. Stitch all around the stocking. Trim the seam allowance to ¼in (6mm). Hem the cuff.

5 Bind all round the stocking with the prepared print fabric strip. Turn in and oversew the raw edges at the top of the stocking.

6 Peel the paper backing from the motifs. Iron in place on the quilted fabric. Seal the edges with fabric glitter paint and allow to dry.

7 Make a hanging loop from ribbon and sew inside the top of the stocking.

Scale: 1 sq = ½in (1cm)

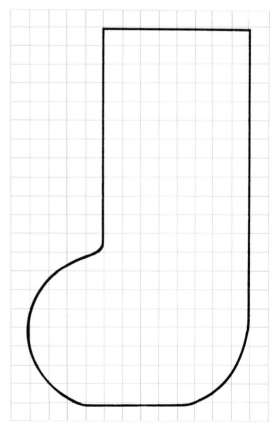

31

Wooden toys

What a thrill to find these little animals hidden in a Christmas stocking! Children will love them and you can adapt the patterns to make other animals.

Materials
3 × 36in (7.5 × 90cm) sheet of ½in
  (1cm)-thick soft balsa wood.
Fine-grade sandpaper
Sanding sealer
Scraps of felt for ears
Thin wool for tails and manes
Wood glue
Latex adhesive
Acrylic paints
Tools: Craft knife; hacksaw blade;
  half-round bastard file

Preparation
1 Trace the patterns and make card templates. Mark in the grain arrows.

2 Position the templates on the wood and draw round the body twice and the head once, making sure that the grain arrows align with the wood grain.

Working the design
3 Cut the shapes out roughly with the craft knife or hacksaw blade. Use the half-round bastard file to shape the pieces.

4 File the flat surfaces of the body pieces back so that when the two bodies are stuck together the legs are about ⅛in (3mm) apart at the feet. Stick the body pieces together.

5 File the head piece to shape, ensuring that the neck edge matches the body edge. Stick the head in place.

> You can also use the animal patterns to make a nursery mobile. Cut the shapes from thick, white cardboard.

6 Round off all edges with the file. Smooth the surface with fine-grade sandpaper. Brush on two coats of sanding sealer, sandpapering again lightly between coats.

7 Paint the animals using the picture as a guide.

8 Cut two ears from brown felt. Pierce ear holes with a thin knitting needle. Fill the hole with latex adhesive and push the bottom of the ear, folded in half with the fold at the back, into the hole.

9 For the tail, wind thin wool 8 times around a piece of card 2in (5cm) wide. Slip the loops from the card and tie together on one side. Pierce a hole in the toy and fill with adhesive. Push the knotted end of the tail in place. Trim the loops off to make the tail.

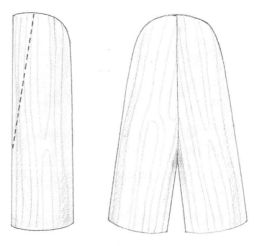

File back the top part of the flat surface of both body pieces so that the legs are ⅛in (3mm) apart.

10 For the mane, wind wool 4 times around a piece of card 1in (2.5cm) wide. Tie the loops on one side. Make four sets of loops. Pierce four holes in the back of the neck. Fill the holes with adhesive and push the wool loops in. When dry, cut the loops, trim the mane and stick it evenly to each side of the neck with some strands coming forward between the ears.

Safety Tips
The animals are not suitable for very young children as balsa wood is a soft wood which can easily be broken or bitten.

Make sure that the safety instructions given on the can are observed when applying the sanding sealer.

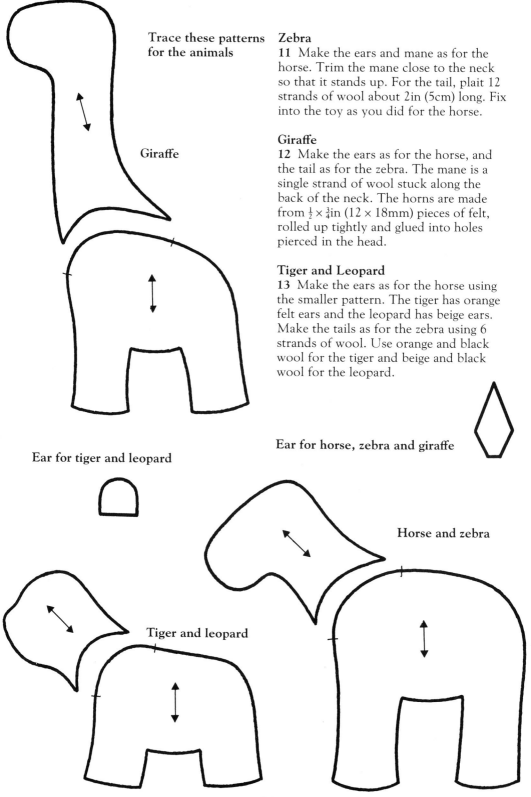

Trace these patterns for the animals

Giraffe

Zebra

11 Make the ears and mane as for the horse. Trim the mane close to the neck so that it stands up. For the tail, plait 12 strands of wool about 2in (5cm) long. Fix into the toy as you did for the horse.

Giraffe

12 Make the ears as for the horse, and the tail as for the zebra. The mane is a single strand of wool stuck along the back of the neck. The horns are made from $\frac{1}{2} \times \frac{3}{4}$in (12 × 18mm) pieces of felt, rolled up tightly and glued into holes pierced in the head.

Tiger and Leopard

13 Make the ears as for the horse using the smaller pattern. The tiger has orange felt ears and the leopard has beige ears. Make the tails as for the zebra using 6 strands of wool. Use orange and black wool for the tiger and beige and black wool for the leopard.

Ear for horse, zebra and giraffe

Ear for tiger and leopard

Horse and zebra

Tiger and leopard

Beanbag toys

Any child would be delighted to discover one of these beany characters in their Christmas stocking. For very young children the toys could be filled with washable toy filling.

SNOWMAN
Materials
Tracing pattern paper
6 × 15in (15 × 38cm) piece of white fleecy
   fabric
Small beans or lentils
Child's striped sock
Small pompons
Red and black stranded embroidery
   cotton
2 small black buttons

Preparation
1 Trace the body and head patterns. Cut out.

2 Cut two 6in (15cm) squares of fleecy fabric and put them right sides together. Pin the body pattern to the 2 layers of fabric. Cut out, ½in (1cm) from the pattern edges.

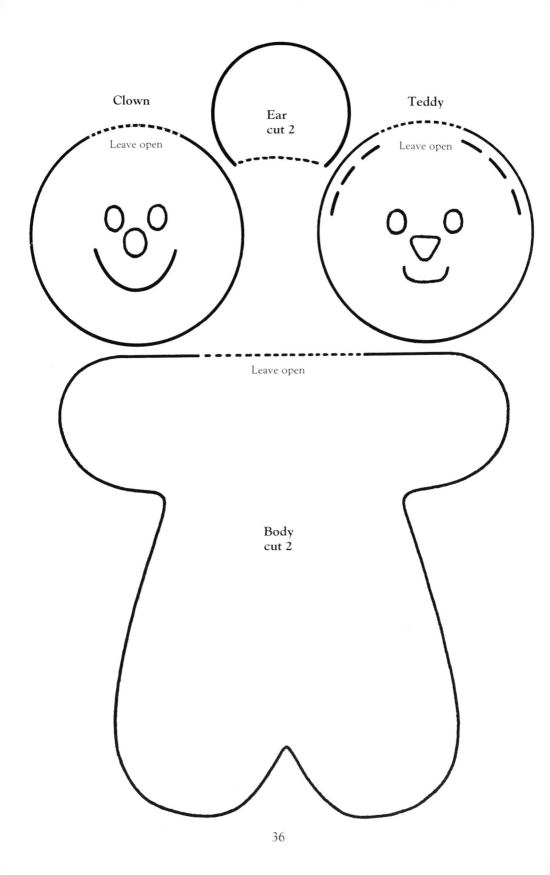

Clown

Ear
cut 2

Teddy

Leave open

Leave open

Leave open

Body
cut 2

36

3 Cut two 3in (7.5cm) squares of fleecy fabric and put them right sides together. Pin the head pattern to the 2 layers of fabric. Cut out, ½in (1cm) from the pattern edges.

4 From the sock, cut a 2 × 5in (5 × 12.5cm) piece with the stripes running lengthways for the hat. For the scarf cut 2 pieces 1½ × 3in (4 × 7.5cm) with the stripes running across the width.

Working the design

5 Stitch the body pieces together taking ½in (1cm) seams and leaving a gap for filling (see pattern). Trim the seams back.

6 Cut Vs under the arms and between the legs to ease and turn right side out.

7 Fold the scarf pieces in half lengthways, right sides together, and stitch ¼in (6mm) from the long edges. Turn the pieces right side out and gather the bottom edges. Sew the top ends of the scarf to the top edge of the body.

8 Stitch the head pieces together taking ½in (1cm) seams and leaving the top edge open. Trim the seams back. Turn right side out. Sew the head to the front of the body, covering the top of the scarf and with the gap in the head seam at the top.

9 Fill the body and the head with small beans or lentils using a paper funnel. Close the seams.

10 Embroider the eyes and nose in satin stitch and the mouth in stem stitch. Sew buttons to the front of the body.

11 With right sides together stitch the short edges of the hat together ¼in (6mm) from the edge. Turn right side out. Fit on to head with the seam at the back. Turn the bottom edge inside the hat and sew in place. Gather the top edges.

12 Sew two wool pompons to the hat and one to the scarf.

TEDDY
Materials
6 × 18in (15 × 45cm) piece of teddy-coloured fleecy fabric
Small beans or lentils
Black stranded embroidery cotton
Small piece of ribbon

Preparation
1 Trace the body, head and ear patterns. Cut out. Cut two 6in (15cm) squares of fleecy fabric and put them right sides together. Pin the body pattern to the 2 layers of fabric. Cut out, ½in (1cm) from the pattern edges. Unpin the pattern.

2 Cut two 3in (7.5cm) squares of fleecy fabric and put them right sides together. Pin the head pattern to the 2 layers of fabric. Cut out ½in (1cm) from the pattern edges. Unpin the pattern.

3 For each ear, cut two 1½in (4cm) squares of fleecy fabric and put them right sides together. Pin the ear pattern to the 2 layers of fabric. Cut out ½in (1cm) from the pattern edges. Unpin the pattern.

Working the design
4 Stitch the body pieces together taking ½in (1cm) seams and leaving a gap for filling (see pattern). Trim the seams back.

5 Cut Vs under the arms and between the legs to ease and turn right side out.

6 Stitch the head pieces together taking ¼in (6mm) seams and leaving the top edge open. Trim the seams. Turn right side out. Sew the head securely to the front of the body with the gap in the head seam at the top. Fill the body and the head with beans. Oversew the openings to close.

7 Stitch the ear pieces together taking ¼in (6mm) seams and leaving the bottom open. Trim the seams. Turn right side out, turn in the raw edges and sew the ears to the head. Embroider the eyes and nose. Sew a ribbon bow under the chin.

Santa puppet

Children love glove puppets and a traditional Santa makes an ideal gift for the Christmas stocking. For a very young child make the pattern smaller and sew on felt eyes and buckle for safety.

Materials
Squared pattern paper
9 × 18in (23 × 45cm) piece of red felt
Scraps of white, black and pink felt
2 small black beads for eyes
Red stranded embroidery cotton
White double-knitting wool
Polyester toy filling
Gold buckle
Latex adhesive

Preparation
1 Draw the body pattern and cut out. Pin to doubled red felt. Mark round the pattern outline. Unpin the pattern. Pin the felt pieces together for stitching.

2 For the head, draw a 3¼in (8cm)-diameter circle on pattern paper. Cut out and pin to doubled pink felt. Mark round the pattern outline. Unpin the pattern. Pin the felt pieces together for stitching.

3 Draw the hat pattern and cut out. Pin to folded red felt. Cut out. Unpin the pattern.

4 To make the white wool curly for the beard, moustache and hair, wind several lengths tightly around knitting needles. Wet the wool and allow to dry on the needles.

Working the design
5 Stitch the body pieces together on the marked line, leaving the straight edges open. Cut out close to the stitching. Cut strips of white felt ⅝in (15mm) wide and stick around the cuffs overlapping the ends at the back. Stick strips down the front of the puppet (see picture).

6 Cut a strip of black felt 11in (28cm) long for the belt. Stick it around the body, overlapping the ends at the back. Spread latex adhesive on the back of the buckle and on the centre of the belt. Allow the adhesive to become tacky, then press the buckle onto the belt.

7 **Head:** Stitch the head pieces together leaving a 2in (5cm) opening at the bottom. Cut out close to the stitching, but leaving about ¼in (6mm) at the opening edges. Stuff the head lightly. With the puppet body on your hand, fit the head in place over the index finger and continue stuffing around your finger using a knitting needle to push the stuffing into the head. Remove the puppet from your hand and sew on the head.

8 **Nose and eyes:** Cut a 1¼in (3cm)-diameter circle of felt for the nose. Gather the edge, pull up, stuff the nose and tie off the thread. Sew on the nose.

9 Make indentations for the eyes by taking a thread tightly through the head in the eye positions (taking care not to sew through the glove part of the puppet). Then sew the bead eyes in place. Use 2 strands of embroidery cotton to work the mouth in stem stitch. Work 1¼in (3cm)-long straight stitches in white wool over the eyes for eyebrows.

10 **Beard and moustache:** Wind a piece of curled wool 80 times around a 1½in (4cm)-wide piece of card. Backstitch across the loops (not through the card) then fold the card lengthways to remove it. Sew the beard loops around the face.

11 The moustache is made in the same way, winding curly wool 6 times around a 2½in (6.5cm)-wide piece of card. Sew the moustache under the nose.

12 The hair is made in the same way from 4 rows of curly wool. Wind each length 50 times around a 1¼in (3cm)-wide piece of card. Sew the hair round the face.

13 Hat: Stitch the long edges together. Trim close to the stitching. Use the pattern to cut out a white felt hat band. Stick in place, overlapping the ends at the seam side. Stitch the hat to the head. Catch the pointed top down. Make a tiny white wool bobble for the end. Sew it on.

Body and hat patterns: scale 1sq = ½in (1cm).

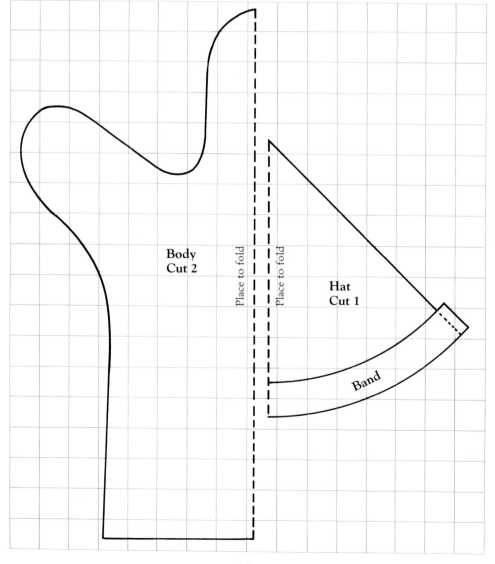

Reindeer mascot

With a piece of magnetic strip on the back this mini reindeer can be stuck to the refrigerator door – or, fastened to a ribbon loop, he can be hung from a child's bag or used for a mobile.

Materials

Squared pattern paper
Beige felt
Dark brown, red and black felt
Scrap of bright-coloured felt for a
    blanket
Scrap of ribbon
Scrap of dark brown wool
Polyester toy filling
Red and black stranded embroidery
    cotton
Fusible web
Tiny bell
Self-adhesive magnetic strip
Latex adhesive

Preparation

1 Draw pattern pieces onto squared
pattern paper and cut them out.

2 Bond 2 pieces of dark brown felt
together with fusible web.

3 Use pattern to cut out 2 antlers from
the double thickness felt, and 2 ears from
beige felt. Pin the head and body patterns
to a double thickness of beige felt and cut
out allowing $\frac{1}{4}$in (6mm) all round.

Working the design

4 Position the antlers and ears between
the layers of felt for the head and hold in
place with a spot of latex adhesive. Stitch
around the head close to the edge, leaving
a gap for filling (see pattern). Stuff the
head lightly and oversew the opening.
Trim the seam allowance close to the
stitching.

5 Stitch around the body outline leaving
a gap in the seam at the neck. Stuff the
legs lightly then stitch the lines of the legs
shown (see the broken lines on the
pattern). Stuff the rest of the body lightly.
Trim the seam allowance close to the
stitching. Sew the head to the neck on
the front of the body. Trim the neck edge
of the head at the back, close to the
stitching.

6 Cut a nose from red felt and stick in
place.

7 Using 2 strands of embroidery thread,
work the eyes in satin stitch and the
mouth in stem stitch.

8 For the mane, wind wool 8 times
around your finger. Tie the loops on one
side and stick to the front of the head
between the ears. Cut the loops and trim
the ends.

9 For the blanket, cut a $1\frac{3}{8} \times 2\frac{1}{2}$in
(3.5 × 6cm) piece of coloured felt. Snip
into the short edges for a fringe, and stick
a piece of ribbon above the fringe,
tucking and gluing the ribbon ends to the
back. Stick the blanket over the back of
the reindeer.

10 Thread a tiny bell through a piece of
narrow ribbon for the collar, overlapping
and sticking the ribbon ends together
behind the neck.

11 Stick a magnetic strip to the back of
the reindeer on the blanket, or make a
hanging loop from the remaining ribbon.

Ideas for the design

The reindeer motif can be used to
make an amusing greeting card. Trace
the shape and cut the head and body
from stiff brown paper, or stick
brown felt to paper and cut out. Cut
the antlers and other details from
contrasting colours and stick them
on. Stick the shape to a piece of
folded, white card. The head could
be cut out separately and fixed on
with a paper fastener so that it is
moveable. Alternatively, the reindeer
could make an amusing place setting
card. Fold white card and stick a
reindeer onto the front. You might
write the guests's name on the
reindeer's coat.

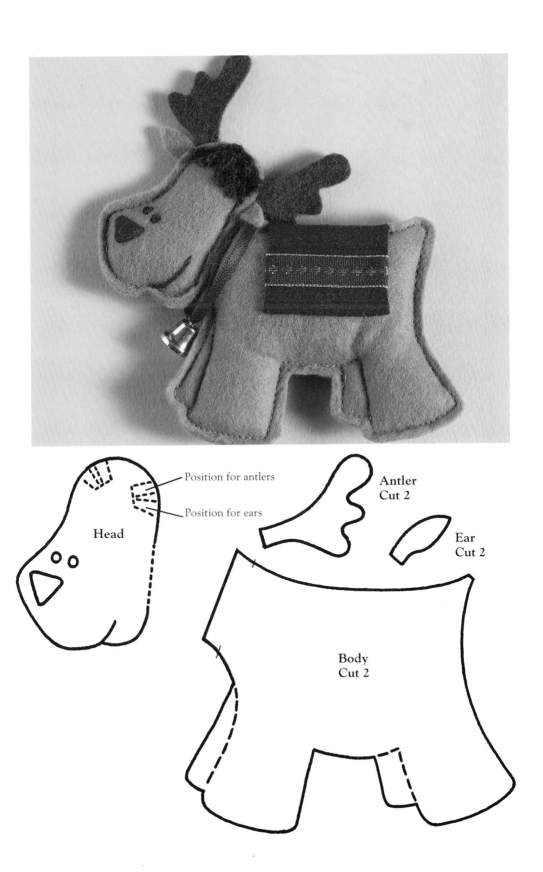

Position for antlers

Position for ears

Head

Antler
Cut 2

Ear
Cut 2

Body
Cut 2

THREE

Specially for the tree

Glittering decos

These dazzling foil decorations will reflect the lights from your tree. They are made from circles and strips of craft foil which has been folded concertina-fashion.

Materials
Craft foil in assorted colours
Cardboard
Narrow ribbon
All-purpose glue

Trace these shapes to make templates

TREE
Preparation
1 Using a pair of compasses, draw a 7in (18cm)-radius circle on green foil. Mark off 24 1¾in (4.5cm) spaces around the edge of the circle. Use the back of a craft knife to score lines from these points to the centre. Cut out the circle and make a cut into the centre along one line.

2 Trace the tree pattern and make a cardboard template.

Working the design
3 Fold the foil circle concertina-fashion.

4 Position the template on one side of the folded foil and draw around.

5 Use a sharp craft knife to cut away the shaded areas (see pattern) through all layers.

6 Stick the end faces together to form the tree.

7 Stick the ends of a piece of ribbon into the centre of the ornament, forming a hanging loop. Dot glue into the centre at the pot end to hold the folds.

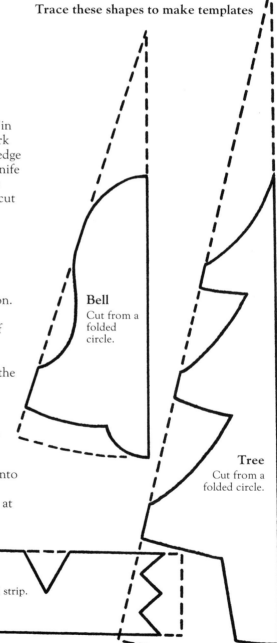

Bell
Cut from a folded circle.

Tree
Cut from a folded circle.

Cracker
Cut from a folded strip.

BELL
Preparation
1 Follow steps 1–2 as given for the tree but using a 4½in (11.5cm)-radius circle of foil, with 18 1½in (4cm) spaces marked around the edge.

Working the design
2 Make as for the tree, using the bell pattern.

CRACKER
Preparation
1 Cut a 12½ × 4½in (31.5 × 11.5cm) strip of foil. Score lines across the width ⅝in (15mm) apart. Trace the cracker pattern and make a cardboard template.

Working the design
2 Fold the strip concertina-fashion.

3 Position the template on one side of the folded foil and draw around. Cut away the shaded areas (see pattern) through all layers.

4 Stick the end faces together and put spots of glue into the centre at each end to hold the ornament together.

5 Stick the ends of a loop of ribbon around the 'waists' of the ornament (see picture).

47

Golden bells

Suffolk puffs are used to make these attractive bells. Each puff is made from a circle of fabric which is gathered around the edge. Children could help to make the puffs.

Materials
(To make 2 bells)
12in (30cm) piece of gold-coloured fabric (44in (112cm)-wide)
Small gold bauble for each bell
12in (30cm) piece of ⅞in (20mm)-wide tartan ribbon
12in (30cm) piece of ⅜in (9mm)-wide tartan ribbon
Latex adhesive

Preparation
1 Cut paper circle templates with the following diameters: 3½in (9cm), 4in (10cm), 5in (12.5cm) and 6in (15cm).

2 Using the templates, for each bell cut circles of gold fabric as follows: 2 × 3½in (9cm), 4 × 4in (10cm), 1 × 5in (12.5cm), 2 × 6in (15cm).

Working the design
3 Fold each circle into quarters and snip off the corner.

4 Cut a 10in (25.5cm) length of narrow tartan ribbon, spread glue on the ends and, using a knitting needle, push the ends into the top of the bauble, leaving a loop about 4½in (11.5cm) long. Leave to dry.

5 Take one of the two largest circles, gather the edges, pull up tightly and fasten off the thread ends.

6 Work the other fabric circles in the same way. The topmost circle, one of the smallest size, is hemmed before gathering the edge.

Assembly
7 Using a knitting needle, push the ribbon loop through each of the puffs in turn, starting with the largest and finishing with the hemmed, smallest. The gathered side is always uppermost. Make a bow with the remaining tartan ribbon using a scrap of the narrow ribbon for the knot and sew to the top of the bell.

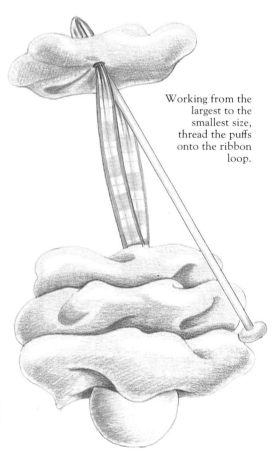

Working from the largest to the smallest size, thread the puffs onto the ribbon loop.

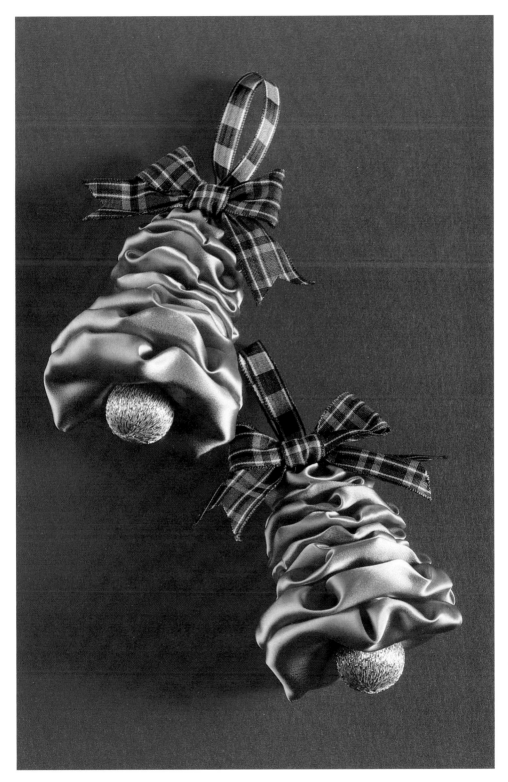

Lacy fairy

This saucy fairy will be popular with young and old alike. Make her for the top of your tree and she may wave her magic wand and make all your wishes come true.

Materials

Pink stockinette
Polyester toy filling
1yd (1m) approximately of 8in (20cm)-wide lace trim
7in (18cm) of 2½in (6cm)-wide pre-gathered broderie anglaise (for pantaloons)
12in (30cm) of 1in (2.5cm)-wide pre-gathered lace (for bodice)
18in (45cm) of thick fuse wire or stem wire
Piece of white stocking or tights
Yellow bouclé wool
Red, pink and black stranded embroidery cottons
Small piece of white felt
Narrow silver braid
Latex adhesive
1 silver pipe-cleaner

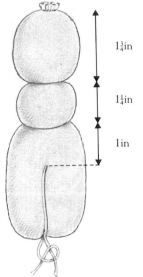

1¾in

1¼in

1in

Bring the needle through and tie the thread ends under the feet to indicate legs.

Working the design

1 For the body, cut a 6½ × 7in (16.5 × 18cm) piece of stockinette with the most stretch across the width. With right sides together, stitch the long edges together taking a 1in (2.5cm) seam (this makes it easier to stitch).

2 Trim the seam allowance and turn the body right side out. Gather around one end close to the edge. Pull up the gathers and tie tightly. Stuff the body firmly, gather the other end and tie tightly.

3 Tie strong threads tightly round the body 1¾in (4.5cm) down from the top for the neck and then a further 1¼in (3cm) down for the waist. Sew the thread ends into the body.

4 With the seam at the back, use a long needle to thread a length of strong thread through the body from front to back 1in (2.5cm) down from the waist. Tie the ends together tightly under the feet to form legs.

5 Tie a thread tightly around the legs ½in (1cm) from the bottom to form feet.

6 **Arms:** Cut two 3½ × 4in (9 × 10cm) pieces of stockinette with the most stretch across the width. Fold each piece in half lengthways. With scissors, round off one end. Right sides together, stitch round taking a 1in (2.5cm) seam and leaving the short, straight edge open. Turn right side out. Stuff the arms. Turn in the raw edges. Oversew the arms to the body. Tie a thread tightly around the arms ½in (1cm) from the bottom to form hands.

7 Using two strands of embroidery cotton, work the open eye in satin stitch and the winking eye, mouth and nose in stem stitch. (Refer to the picture for colours.)

8 Wings: Bend a 9in (23cm) piece of wire into a circle twisting the ends together. Stretch a piece of white stocking fabric over the wire circle so that it is covered on both sides. Bind thread around the excess fabric over the twisted wire ends to hold it in place. Trim neatly. Form into the wing shape (see picture). Make 2 wings. Sew the wings to the back of the figure.

9 Pantaloons: With right sides together, stitch the short edges of the broderie anglaise. Turn right side out and run a gathering thread along the top (pregathered) edge. Fit over the figure with the seam at the back and tie the gathers tightly at the waist. Sew the front and back of the broderie anglaise to the legs to look like pantaloons.

10 With right sides together, join the short edges of the wide lace for the skirt. Fold the skirt in half all around with the right side out. Sew a gathering thread along the folded edge. Fit over the figure, pull up gathers to fit around the waist and tie tightly.

11 The bodice is made from the narrow pre-gathered lace wrapped round the body. Start at the front, taking the lace ends round the waist to the back. Cross the ends and take them over the shoulders to the front. Oversew the ends together to make a V neck. Sew the bottom of the bodice to the top of the skirt.

12 Hair: Wind wool 70 times round a $3\frac{1}{2}$in (9cm)-wide piece of card. Tie the loops on one side. With the tied part in the centre, allow the loops to spread out. Position the hair on the figure with the knot loosely at the top. Tie a piece of wool around the hair approximately $\frac{1}{2}$in (1cm) from the knot to form a bun.

13 Spread latex adhesive over the head and stick the hair in place. Cut the loops and trim the hair to shape.

14 Make sandals with a piece of white felt cut to the shape of the soles of the feet. Stick in place and stick on pieces of silver thread to represent straps.

15 Finish the fairy with a piece of silver thread around her bun and the neck edge of the bodice. Bend the silver pipe-cleaner into a wand with a star on top and stick it to her hand.

Tie the fabric over the wire circle.

Cross the bodice lace at the back.

Bring the lace ends to the front to form a V-neck.

Christmas folk

Add the finishing touch to your tree with these festive toy figures. They are embroidered on plastic canvas, which is a relatively new craft, but very easy to do.

Materials

Plastic canvas, 10 holes to 1in (2.5cm)
Tapestry (or knitting) wool in black,
   white, red, blue, gold, pink and brown
Small pieces of felt
Narrow ribbon

Preparation

1 For each decoration cut a 3 × 4in
(7.5 × 10cm) piece of plastic canvas.

Working the design

2 Each square on the charts represents
one half cross stitch worked over an
intersection of canvas. Work the
embroideries following the charts. The
soldier's and teddy's eyes are French
knots and the clown and teddy's noses
are a single cross stitch. The clown's eyes,
all outline stitches and soldier's and
teddy's mouths are worked in backstitch
using a single, separated strand of black
wool. The clown's mouth is also worked
in backstitch, but using the complete
thickness of red wool.

3 Cut away the excess canvas around the
worked design. Overcast the edges,
matching wool colours, (except the
soldier's epaulettes and teddy's paws and
ears which are worked in gold). The top
of the clown's hat is worked in blue.

4 Sew the ends of a ribbon loop to the
back of the figure for a hanger.

5 Using the ornament as a template, cut
a piece of felt, slightly smaller in size, and
sew it neatly to the back.

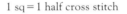

1 sq = 1 half cross stitch

Soldier

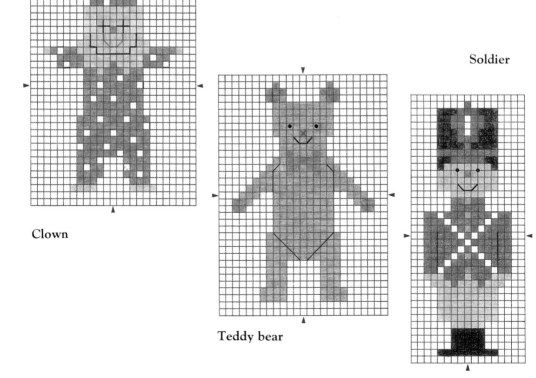

Clown

Teddy bear

Baubles and bows

These colourful decorations are made from coloured plastic bags. They are very simple and ideal for children to make – and, of course, help to recycle waste materials.

Materials

Plastic bags in different colours
Silver thread
Double-sided tape
Thin cardboard (such as a cereal packet)

Baubles

1 Cut two 1¼in (3cm)-radius circles from cardboard. Cut a ⅜in (9mm)-radius circle from the middle of each to make rings.

2 Cut strips of plastic bag approximately 1in (2.5cm) wide.

3 Hold the two rings together. Wind the strips around the rings using a different colour for each of three layers.

4 When the hole in the middle is almost filled, cut through the plastic strands around the edge of the rings. Tie a piece of silver thread around the 'waist' of the ornament between the cardboard rings and tie tightly. Tie the ends to make a hanging loop.

5 Tear and remove the cardboard rings. Trim the ball to shape.

Bows

6 Cut a 1¼in × 15in (3 × 38cm) piece of plastic bag. Fold the ends to the middle, crossing them. Gather across the middle through all layers. Leaving the needle and thread still attached, pull up gathers and tie off tightly.

7 Cut a narrow strip of plastic in another colour and wind this around the centre, sewing it in place at the back. Thread silver thread through the back to make a hanging loop. Trim the bow's tails.

Mini-wreaths

8 Cut three strips of different coloured plastic bags 3 × 16in (7.5 × 40cm). Tie the ends together with silver thread, leaving long ends of thread.

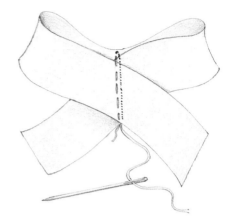

Gather across the middle of the folded strip.

Tie a thread around the overlapped plait ends.

9 Plait the strips, bending the plait into a curve as you go. When there is only about 1in (2.5cm) of the strips left, bring the two ends of the plait together to make a circle, crossing the ends.

10 Tie the thread around the overlapping ends. Make a hanging loop. Spread out the plastic ends into a fan shape.

Chains

11 Cut strips ¾ × 4in (2 × 10cm). Join a strip with double-sided tape. Thread the next piece through the ring and join the ends with tape. Continue, threading on each piece to form the chain.

Not-so-heavenly choir

These little choristers can be displayed in a window or on a shelf grouped round a candle. A line of them might be arranged down the middle of a party table.

Materials

(For one chorister)
Tracing pattern paper
Thin cardboard
Table tennis ball
Red cartridge paper
White bond paper
White crêpe paper
Scrap of black paper
Flesh-coloured poster (or acrylic) paint
Double knitting wool; silver thread
Latex adhesive

Preparation

1 Pierce a hole in the ball and use the point of a pencil to enlarge it to about ¼in (6mm) diameter.

2 Trace arm pattern and make a cardboard or paper template. Cut two arms from white paper. Paint the ends (for the hands) and the table tennis ball flesh-coloured.

Working the design

3 Draw a 4½in (11cm)-radius circle on the red paper. Use a protractor to divide the circumference into three (120° each). Cut out the three segments (each will make the cassock for one figure). Form the segment into a cone, overlapping the edges and gluing them about 1in (2.5cm) at the base.

4 Draw a 3¾in (9.5cm)-radius semicircle on white paper with an inner semicircle of 1in (2.5cm) radius. With a protractor, measure an angle of 144° from the horizontal. Cut out the segment. Form the paper into a cone to make a surplice which will fit loosely over the cassock, overlapping the edges and gluing about 1in (2.5cm) at the base. Stick the seam of the surplice to the seam of the cassock.

5 For sleeves, cut a 2in (5cm)-radius semicircle of white paper. Cut into two halves. Form each half into a cone overlapping and gluing about ½in (1cm) at the bottom. Flatten the cone slightly and glue the arm up into the sleeve. Stick the sleeves to the sides of the body.

Trace these patterns for the arms and features

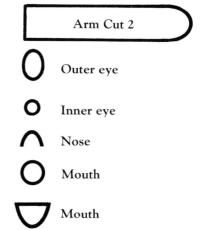

Arm Cut 2

Outer eye

Inner eye

Nose

Mouth

Mouth

58

6 Stick the head onto the neck of the cassock.

7 For hair, wind wool 40 times around a piece of card 2¼in (5.5cm) wide. Slip the loops from the card and tie together on one side. Cut the loops opposite the knot. Spread the top, back and sides of the head with latex adhesive. Place the knot on top of the head and spread the 'hair' around the back, sides and front. Trim the ends to shape. Make a silver thread hanging loop and sew to the back of the hair near the crown of the head.

8 Cut eyes and mouth from white and black paper and stick in place. Draw a nose with a fibretip pen.

9 For the ruffle cut a 1¼ × 7½in (3 × 19cm) strip of crêpe paper with the grain running crossways. Fold in half lengthways. Run a gathering thread along the fold line, pull up the gathers and tie around the neck.

10 Make a book of carols from a 1 × 1½in (2.5 × 4cm) piece of red paper folded in half, with an inner page cut slightly smaller from white paper. The comic is made in the same way with 'cartoons' drawn in coloured pens. Stick the hands to the book.

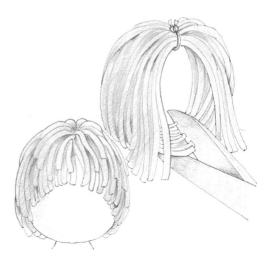

Cut the wool loops and glue the knot to the top of head.

The figure could also be adapted to make an angel. Make the skirt cone in gold card with an overskirt cut from a lace doyley. Cut wings a gold lace doyley and stick them to the back. Stick a gold paper star to the forehead. Give the angel a smiling face.

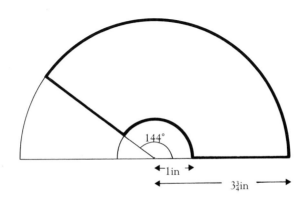

Make the surplice from this diagram pattern.

59

Musical tree trims

Nicely mellowed sheet music makes original and attractive decorations. Try using a musical theme for all your tree decorations, adding choirboys and bells.

Materials
Old sheet music
Narrow red ribbon
Small fir cones sprayed gold
Modelling clay which can be oven-baked
Gold paint for painting clay
Gold thread
All-purpose glue
Contact glue (or a glue gun)

Preparation
1 Roll a piece of modelling clay to approximately $\frac{1}{8}$in (3mm) diameter. Bend into a treble clef shape directly on a baking sheet. Slip small pieces of card under the edges to stop the sides sagging. Bake, following the manufacturer's instructions. Paint the pieces gold.

2 Trim the music sheets to tidy the edges if necessary.

Working the design
Scrolls
3 Cut a sheet of music to 4in (10cm) long and $7\frac{1}{2}$in (19cm) wide. Roll and glue into a tube about $1\frac{1}{4}$in (3cm) in diameter.

4 Wind narrow red ribbon around the centre of the tube and secure with glue.

5 Make a bow with long tails. Position the treble clef on the tails (refer to the picture) and sew in place by catching threads over it in a few places. Stick the bow at an angle to the centre of the scroll. Make a hanging loop from gold thread and sew (or glue) in place so that the scroll hangs at an angle with the treble clef hanging vertically.

Fans
6 Cut a sheet of music to $6\frac{1}{2}$in (16cm) long by $7\frac{1}{2}$in (19cm) wide. Fold from the bottom concertina-fashion, taking approximately $\frac{3}{4}$in (18mm) folds to make a fan.

Support the treble clef on the baking tray with cardboard scraps to prevent it from sagging.

Tie the fan at the bottom. Stick the pleat faces together.

7 Fold the fan in half. Hold the two halves together and wind narrow red ribbon around the bottom of the fan about ½in (12mm) from the fold. Glue the end securely. Stick the two centre edges of the fan together.

8 Make a red ribbon bow and stick this to the bottom of the fan. Make a hanging loop from red ribbon.

Cones

9 Cut a sheet of music to 4in (10cm) long and 7½in (19cm) wide. Roll and glue into a cone shape.

10 Use contact glue (or a glue gun) to stick gold fir cones into the music cone.

11 Make a small bow for the front and stick it on. Make a hanging loop from narrow red ribbon.

Soft hearts

Little heart wreaths made from card covered with Christmas print fabric make lovely tree decorations. Hang tiny bells or baubles from the centre to add extra sparkle.

Materials
Tracing pattern paper
Thick card
Christmas print fabric, 44in (112cm) wide
White ribbon
Silver thread
Sticky tape

Preparation
1 Trace the heart shape on folded paper. Transfer the heart shape onto thick card. Cut out. (One card heart is required for each decoration.) Cut the heart through where indicated with a broken line (see pattern).

2 Cut a 3in (7.5cm) strip of fabric across the width of the fabric. Fold in half along the length with right sides together.

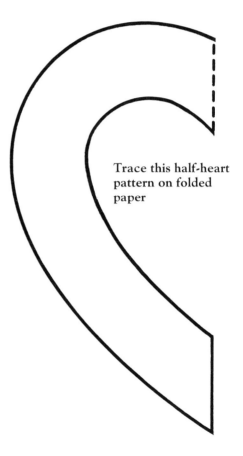

Trace this half-heart pattern on folded paper

Ease the fabric tube onto the card heart.

Starting 2in (5cm) from one end, stitch along the length, ½in (1cm) from the raw edges, to within 2in (5cm) from the other end. Trim the seam allowance and turn the tube right side out.

Working the design
3 With the seam at the back, ease the fabric tube over the card, spreading the gathers evenly.

4 When all the fabric is on the card, push the fabric at the bottom aside so that the bottom of the card heart is visible. Rejoin the cut edges of the card heart with sticky tape. Cut off the unstitched ends of the fabric tube, turn in the raw edges overlapping them and oversew the join neatly.

5 Make a ribbon bow and stitch in place.

6 Make a hanging loop from silver thread and stitch to the back of the heart.

Christmas geese

Dressed in their tartan bows, these geese are delightful toys but also make a cheerful addition to the tree. They are made from stretchy towelling socks.

Materials
(For two geese)
Squared pattern paper
Large white stretch-towelling sock
Polyester toy filling
Scraps of orange and black felt
Scrap of fusible web
18in (45cm) of ⅜in (15mm)-wide tartan ribbon
8in (20cm) of ⅜in (9mm)-wide tartan ribbon
Silver thread
Latex adhesive

Preparation
1 Draw the body, beak and foot shapes on squared paper and cut out for patterns.

2 Sandwich fusible web between two layers of orange felt. Use the pattern to cut out two feet and one beak for each goose. Cut eyes from single black felt.

Working the design
3 Turn the sock inside out. Pin the body pattern to the sock through both thicknesses. (Position it so that another goose can be made from the same sock.)

4 Stitch around the pattern leaving a gap on the goose's back (see pattern). Cut out about ¼in (6mm) from the stitching and about ½in (1cm) from the back gap. Remove the pattern. Snip into the curves to ease the seams. Turn right side out.

5 Stuff the goose lightly and oversew the opening to close.

6 Stick the beak and feet in position with adhesive.

7 Put a needle and strong white thread through the head where the eyes are to be positioned and sew through the head a few times, pulling tightly so that an indentation is made on each side of the head. Sew the felt eyes in position in the indentations.

8 Stick a strip of narrow tartan ribbon around the neck like a collar. Make a bow with the wider ribbon. Cut a small piece of the narrow ribbon and stick it round the waist of the bow. Sew the bow to the collar.

Scale: 1 sq = ½in (1cm)

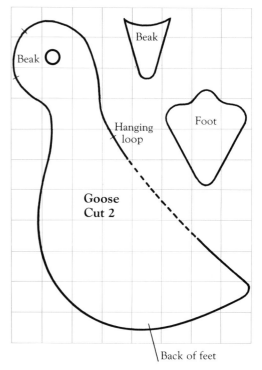

64

9 Sew a silver thread hanging loop to the top of the back, so that the goose balances correctly when hanging. For a different look, you might give each goose a necklet of tiny pearl beads, instead of a tartan ribbon bow.

FOUR

Set the table

Buffet table decoration

This sparkling arrangement is designed for a buffet, but it would look equally attractive on the dinner table. Complete the display with the matching napkin rings.

Materials
6 × 12in (15 × 30cm) shallow basket
1½ blocks of florists' dry foam
5 gold 9½ (24cm) candles
5 candle holders
Dried material as follows:
Hydrangea heads
Green broom bloom
Atracxa
Honesty
Pink helichrysum heads
5 poppy seed heads
Green briza segromi
Gold spray paint
All-purpose glue (or a glue gun)

Preparation
1 Spray the atracxa and poppy seed heads gold.

2 Cut the half block of foam into half again and stick both pieces onto the whole block. Push the complete block into the basket and stick in place.

3 Insert two candle holders into the top 'step', one into the middle 'step' and two into the lower 'step' of foam.

4 Wire the flower heads so that they have 2 'legs'

Working the design
5 Insert the briza segromi and atracxa into the foam around the base and at the back of the basket to give height and shape.

6 Fill in with hydrangea heads, broom bloom, honesty and poppy seed heads so that the foam is completely covered. (Refer to the picture.)

7 Insert helichrysum heads at intervals. Then insert the candles.

Fix the two quarter blocks to the full-sized block of foam.

Safety tip
Care should be taken with candles as dried materials are highly inflammable. Never leave lighted candles unattended and replace them with new ones when they have burned about halfway down.

$\frac{1}{4}$ block

$\frac{1}{4}$ block

1 block

Lacy tree

This pretty little table tree would make an ideal gift or an attractive table centre. Fill it with Christmas pot pourri and your room will be filled with fragrance.

Materials
12in (30cm) square of dark green fabric
Polyester toy filling
Pot pourri (optional)
4yd (4m) approximately of pre-gathered white and silver lace, 1½in (37mm) wide
10in (25cm) piece of silver ribbon, 1in (2.5cm) wide
3½in (9cm) square of dark green felt
Latex adhesive

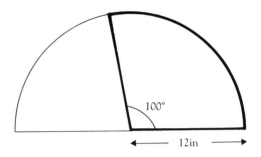

Draw this pattern for the tree. Use the shaded section.

Preparation
1 Draw a 12in (30cm)-radius semicircle on a piece of thin paper. Use a protractor to mark 100° on the semicircle and cut out this section. Use this section as a pattern to cut the green fabric.

Working the design
2 Fold the fabric in half, right sides together, and stitch the straight edges, taking a ½in (1cm) seam. Trim the seam allowance and turn right side out.

3 Stuff the shape firmly (or fill with pot pourri) to about 3in (7.5cm) from the base. Run a gathering thread about ¼in (6mm) from the bottom edge. Pull up gathers, inserting more stuffing to fill the shape and tie off the thread ends.

4 Starting at the bottom, sew pre-gathered lace in a spiral around the tree – as you work up the tree add extra gathers in the lace to prevent the ungathered edge from being pulled in too tightly. Finish off at the top neatly.

5 Make a ribbon bow and sew it to the top of the tree. Cut a circle of felt and stick to the base.

Sew the lace in a spiral round the tree

Icicles for the lacy tree
Thread tiny silver and clear glass beads on fine wire, with one or two silver sequins between. Twist the wire ends through the lace edges to hang.

Reindeer holiday cloth

This cross stitch design can be used to decorate all your Christmas table linen. Use it for napkins or a breadbasket cloth. You could also work the motifs on the corners of a tablecloth.

Materials

18in (45cm) square of 14 count evenweave fabric

Stranded embroidery cottons, tan, dark tan, red, black and gold; short lengths of white, pink, yellow, blue and green

Preparation

1 Machine-stitch the fabric all round ½in (1cm) from the raw edges. Count threads, referring to the chart, to position the embroidery. You will find it easiest to start with the sleigh, 75 threads from the left hand edge, and 4 threads up.

Working the embroidery

2 Using 2 strands of embroidery cotton throughout, work the sleigh, Santa, reindeer, and parcels from the chart using cross stitch and three-quarter cross stitch.

3 Work the stars in double cross stitch using gold threads. Work the eyes in black French knots.

4 Work the outlines, antlers and reins in backstitch, using a single strand of black.

Finishing

5 To fringe the edges, unravel the fabric back to the machine-stitched lines. Alternatively, the edges of the cloth could be bound with a purchased bias binding, in bright red or green.

Binding raw edges

Napkins and cloths made from loosely-woven embroidery fabric can either have fringed edges or they can be bound with bias binding. To do this, unfold one edge of the prepared binding and lay it against the fabric with right sides facing. Baste, then stitch along the crease. Trim the fabric edge a little and fold the binding over the edge to the wrong side. Baste, then slipstitch in place, working over the previous stitches.

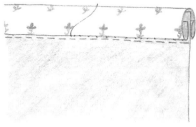

Open the binding, baste, then stitch along the fold-line.

Fold the binding to the wrong side and slipstitch in place.

1 sq = 1 cross stitch

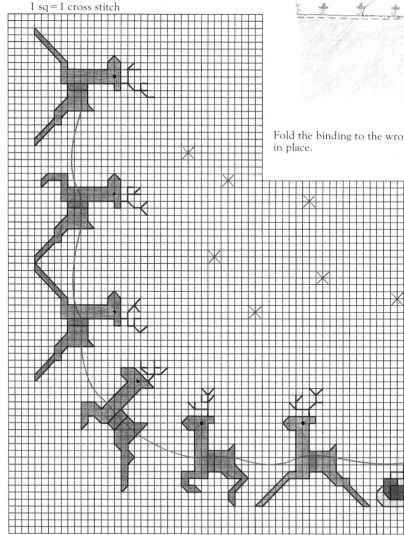

Happy snowman

Standing about 24in (60cm) tall, this jolly fellow will take pride of place at your party table. The head just rests in place so the body can be filled with small gifts for all the family.

Materials

Newspaper torn into small squares
3 pints (1½ litres) of prepared wallpaper
   paste
1 large balloon
1 smaller balloon
White emulsion paint
1yd (1m) approximately of medium-
   thickness polyester wadding
Child's party hat, painted black
14 × 20in (35 × 50cm) piece of tartan
   fabric
Red oven-baked modelling clay; clay
   varnish
8in (20cm) piece of ⅛in (3mm)-diameter
   wood dowel
Red pen or paint
2 black buttons for eyes
Orange and red felt
Piece of ¾in (18mm)-wide red ribbon (long
   enough to go around the hat)
Sprig of holly sprayed gold
Latex adhesive

Preparation

1 Inflate the balloons so that the smaller
head looks in proportion to the larger
body. Cover the surface with at least four
layers of small squares of paper soaked in
paste to within about 1in (2.5cm) of the
neck of the balloon. Allow to dry for
several days with the large balloon
standing on its bottom (neck upwards) so
that the bottom dries flat to form a base.
Once the top has dried, turn it on its side
to allow the bottom to dry.

2 When dry, pierce the balloons and
allow the air to escape slowly, then
remove them. Trim the neck edge of the
body back neatly so that a hand will fit
inside, and trim the neck edge of the
head so that it fits over the neck of the
body.

3 Paint both head and body with
emulsion paint, so that the newsprint
does not show through. Leave to dry.

4 For the umbrella handle, roll a strip of
modelling clay to about ⅜in (9mm)
diameter. Form it into a curve, round off

Stand the balloon on its bottom so that it dries
flat to form a base.

one end and add a strip of clay around
the other end. Push the dowel about 1in
(2.5cm) up into the wider end and bake
according to the manufacturer's
instructions. Paint the end of the dowel.

Working the design

5 Cover the head and body with
wadding. The best way to do this is to
tear pieces of wadding to cover a section
at a time. Spread latex adhesive on the
surface and press the wadding in place.
Any overlapping pieces can be torn off.

6 Arms: Cut 2 pieces of wadding
6½ × 13in (16.5 × 33cm). Round off one
end for the hand and tear the other end
for the shoulder. Fold the long edges
together so that one overlaps the other
by about 1in (2.5cm). Sew together from
the shoulder end and run a gathering
thread around the curved end. Pull up
the gathers to form the hand. Stuff the
arms lightly with scraps of wadding and
stick in position. (Refer to the picture for
the position.) Pin while drying.

7 Trace the nose pattern and cut out
from orange felt. Fold and stitch the long
edge. Turn right side out and stuff with
scraps of wadding. Run a gathering
thread around the end about ¼in (6mm)
from the edge, pull up and tie off. Mark

black lines on the nose to represent a carrot. Stick the nose in position. Trace and cut out the mouth in red felt and stick in place. Sew the eyes in position, taking the thread through the wadding and the papier mâché core.

8 Wrap red ribbon around the hat, sticking the overlapping ends together at the back. Stick a sprig of holly to the side of the hat.

9 Make a bow tie from a 5 × 10in (12.5 × 25.5cm) piece of tartan fabric sewn into a tube. Wrap a 2½in × 5in (6.5 × 12.5cm) piece round for the knot. Sew the bow tie in place.

10 For the umbrella, draw a 13in (33cm)-diameter circle on tracing paper. Fold it in half three times to divide it into eight equal segments. Open the paper. Draw a line from each point on the circumference of the circle to the next to make an octagon. Pin the octagonal pattern to a piece of tartan fabric. Draw around using a soft pencil. Mark the centre point. Cut out ¼in (6mm) from the outside line.

11 Machine-stitch across the octagon from the centre to the points. Zig-zag-stitch around the edges on the marked line. Trim close to the zig-zag stitching. Press the shape to form umbrella spokes. Make a small hole in the middle of the shape. Fit the end of the dowel through, securing it in place with spots of adhesive. Take a stitch through the umbrella at the octagon points and tie the thread ends tightly to the dowel just below the handle. Stick the umbrella over the snowman's arm.

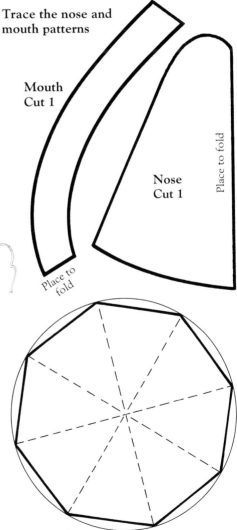

Trace the nose and mouth patterns

Mouth
Cut 1

Nose
Cut 1

Place to fold

Place to fold

Draw an octagon for the umbrella like this

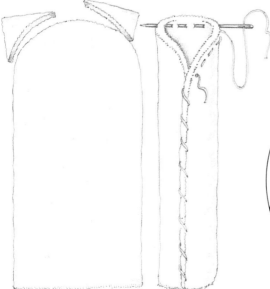

Arms: Round off one end for the hand, oversew the overlap together, gather the curved end.

77

Appliqué candle

Here is a simple way of decorating plain candles to give them a festive look – just cut shapes from modelling wax and fix them on. Trace the motifs here or choose some from giftwrap paper.

Materials
Red candle 6 × 3in (15 × 7.5cm)
Sheet of green modelling wax

Preparation
1 Draw the design for the appliqué motif onto a piece of paper and cut out. (Check that the design is appropriate to the size and diameter of the candle you are using.)

Working the design
2 Place the paper cutout on the modelling wax and trace around it with a felt tip pen.

3 Cut out the shape, using a craft knife.

4 Warm one side with a hairdryer until the modelling wax is sticky to the touch.

5 Position the appliqué on the side of the candle and gently press down the edges with the fingers. Leave to cool.

Press the wax appliqué onto the candle.

Trace these shapes for candle appliqué.

Pleated paper tree

This little table tree is easy to construct and costs very little to make. Patterned Christmas giftwrap looks bright and festive, but plain paper to match a room scheme could also be used.

Materials
2 sheets of giftwrap
Cartridge paper
Small pot, spray-painted gold
12in (30cm) of wood dowel, ⅜in (9mm) diameter
Decorators' filler or modelling clay to weight the pot
Contact glue (or a glue gun)
1yd (1m) approximately of narrow ribbon

Preparation
1 Cut 3 circles of giftwrap 12in (30cm), 13in (33cm) and 14in (35.5cm) in diameter. On each circle, draw a line from the centre to the circumference and cut along the line.

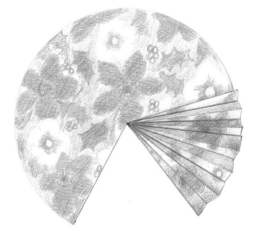

Pleat the marked and scored circles of giftwrap.

2 Cut 3 semicircles of cartridge paper 5½in (14cm), 6in (15cm) and 6½in (16.5cm) radius. Overlap and glue the edges to make cones measuring approximately 4½in (11.5cm), 5¼in (13.5cm) and 6in (15cm) in diameter at the base. (These cones, which will be hidden, support the outer pleated paper cones.) Cut off the tops of the larger two so that they fit neatly over the dowel.

Stick the largest pleated cone over the paper cone; slip onto the dowel tree trunk.

3 Fix the dowel vertically in the pot using filler or modelling clay to hold it securely.

Working the design
4 Using a pair of compasses, measure and mark 1in (2.5cm) spaces around the edges on the back of the smallest giftwrap circle. Gently score lines from these points to the centre.

5 Fold along the lines concertina-fashion. Glue the free edges together to make a cone.

6 With the pleats spread evenly, stick the pleated cone over the smallest of the cartridge paper cones.

7 Repeat the process with the other two circles, using 1⅛in (28mm) spaces for the middle-sized circle and 1¼in (3cm) spaces for the largest circle. Cut off the top of the two largest pleated cones so that they too fit neatly over the dowel.

8 Position each cone on to the dowel, starting with the largest, and secure each in place with contact glue.

9 Make a ribbon bow with long tails for the top of the tree. Fix a smaller one for the pot.

FIVE

Christmas workshop

Great little character toys

The children will have fun making little people out of cardboard tubes and coloured paper. You could adapt the designs to make characters for a toy theatre or a nativity scene.

Materials
Cardboard tubes approximately 4½in
    (11.5cm) long, 1¾in (4.5cm) diameter
Coloured paper and thin card
Felt tip pens
Scraps of braid, Lurex, foil etc
All-purpose glue

Preparation
1 Trace the feet, arm and ear patterns and make card templates.

Working the design
Basic Figure
2 Each tube is covered with 6in (15cm) strips of paper which are wrapped around the tube, overlapped and glued at the back to represent the head, shirt, trousers, skirt or legs etc.

3 Cut out two arms in the same colour as the face. Cut out sleeves where necessary and stick on to arms. Add any accessories or stripes and draw fingers on the hands. Roll the arm into a tube on a pencil and stick the overlap. Stick arms to the sides of the body.

4 Draw the hair and features or use coloured paper using the picture as a guide. If ears are required, cut these from the same coloured paper as the face. Make a small slit on each side of the head with a craft knife and fit the ears in place, sticking tabs inside the tube.

5 Add any accessories.

6 Cut the feet from card and stick to the tube.

Clown
7 Use felt tip pens to draw the checks on the trousers and the spots on the bow tie. Add braces.

Indian
8 Extend the face colour to cover chest. Use felt tip pens to draw the lines on the breastplate, the tassles down the sides of the trousers and stitching on the moccasins. Add feathers and a loincloth.

Pirate
9 Cover the top and bottom of the tube with the face-coloured paper. Draw hairs on the arms and a tattoo. Make the knife from thin card covered in foil.

Lady Soldier
10 Cover the top and bottom of the tube with the face-coloured paper, with uniform colour for the centre. Cut a triangular piece of white paper for the shirt, stick on a piece of black paper cut into a tie shape and mark on lapels. Stick the shirt to the top of the uniform. Mark the hair with a felt tip pen and add a strip of narrow uniform-coloured paper for the hat over a semicircle of the same colour for the peak.

Making cardboard tubes
Use a flexible cardboard. Cut a hole in a piece of cardboard the diameter of the desired tube. Cut a piece of card to the desired depth. Roll it up and fit into the hole. Allow it to fill the hole and mark the overlap. Remove the cardboard and glue the overlap.

Convict

11 Paint a paper ball black and fix it to a short length of silver-coloured chain. Cut small paper ears and stick them either side of the head..

Opera Singer

12 Extend the face-coloured paper to half the tube. Make a scalloped top for the dress before sticking in place. Add scraps of braid for the bracelet, tiara and slippers.

Feet

Ear

Tab

Arm

Cut along broken
line for sleeve

Nose

Eye

Clown's braces
Cut 2

Eye patch

Clown's bow tie

Pirate's knife

Front

Indian's hair
Cut 2

Indian's breastplate

These shapes will help you to dress
the character dolls.

Christmas robin picture

Embroider this plump robin for a Christmas picture and you will probably want to display it all year. The picture could make a lovely present for someone special.

Materials

12in (30cm) square of fine, white
   embroidery fabric
Skein of dark green stranded embroidery
   cotton
Crewel wool – dark brown, mid-brown,
   light brown, beige, black, white,
   orange, orange-red and yellow-green;
Crewel needle

Preparation

1 Trace the pattern and transfer the
design to the fabric.

Working the embroidery

2 Using two strands of embroidery
cotton, work the holly leaves in satin
stitch. Work the under leaves in yellow-
green crewel wool. Work the veins in a
single strand of crewel wool in stem
stitch.

3 Using two strands of crewel wool
together, work the rest of the embroidery
following the key for colours and
stitches.

Finishing

4 Press lightly on the back to 'emboss'
the embroidery.

5 The embroidery can be displayed in a
7in (18cm) flexi-frame.

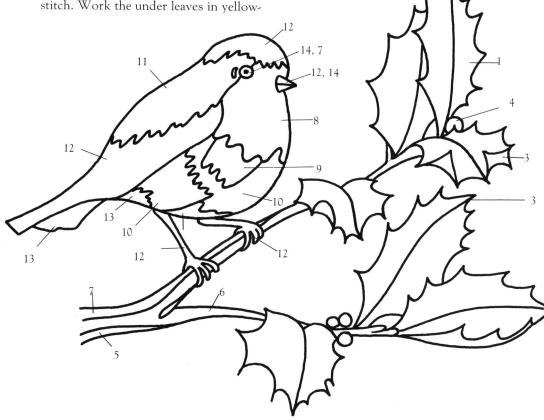

Key: 1 Dark green stranded cotton, satin stitch;
2 Yellow-green wool, satin stitch; **3** Yellow-
green wool, single strand, stem stitch; **4** Orange-
red wool, satin stitch; **5** Dark brown wool, long
and short stitch; **6** Mid-brown wool, long and
short stitch; **7** White wool, long and short
stitch; **8** Orange-red wool, long and short stitch;
9 Orange wool, long and short stitch; **10** Beige
wool, long and short stitch; **11** Light brown wool,
long and short stitch; **12** Mid-brown wool, long
and short stitch; **13** Dark brown wool, long and
short stitch; **14** Black wool.

Desert scene greeting card

Different grades of sandpaper are used to make this unusual greeting card. The method can be adapted for any silhouette – you could trace a suitable picture from an old Christmas card.

Materials

$8\frac{1}{2} \times 18$in (21×45cm) piece of thin card in blue or black

Tracing paper

4 different grades of sandpaper, fine, medium grade, medium-to-coarse, coarse

Old pair of scissors

Star sequins, one large, several small

Piece of thin white card (for the scroll)

Gold glitter pen

All-purpose glue

Preparation

1 Draw a pencil line across the card 2½in (6.5cm) from one short end.

2 Trace the camel and wise men (the rein is added later), and transfer the tracing onto the card so that the feet rest on the pencilled line.

Working the design

3 With a sharp craft knife, and working on a protected surface, cut around the figures (except under the feet). Remove the paper shown shaded on the pattern. Score along the pencilled line (except under the feet).

4 Draw, then score a line across the card 2½in (6.5cm) from the first line (except where it crosses the camel). Draw, then score a third line 6½in (16.5cm) from the second line.

5 Carefully fold the card concertina-fashion so that the figures remain upright.

6 Select the finest grade sandpaper for the most distant dunes. Cut out a piece the width of the card and about 2½in (6.5cm) deep. Cut a wavy line along one long edge to represent dunes. Position on the card, but do not glue in place until the other dunes have been cut out and positioned.

The finest grade sandpaper is the distant dunes. The coarses grade goes on the foreground.

Cut around the figures then measure and mark the fold lines. Score across them.

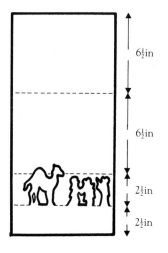

6½in

6½in

2½in

2½in

90

7 Cut out the other dunes in the same way using the medium grade next and the medium-to-coarse grade for the dunes immediately behind the figures. This should be cut deep enough to extend to the bottom of the card, covering the holes left by the camel's head and hump.

8 Use the coarsest grade for the foreground, cutting the top unevenly so that a small amount of card is revealed under the figures for shadows.

9 Stick all the layers of sandpaper in position.

10 Draw a scroll on white card for your Christmas message and stick in place. Decorate the edge with glitter.

11 Finish the card with a line of glitter around the edge. Cut out a curved strip of card for the reins and stick in position. Stick sequin stars in the sky.

Trace these figures for the desert scene

Cross stitched greeting cards

Anyone will love to receive one of these jolly characters. They can be embroidered in an evening and after Christmas they could be framed and used to decorate a child's room.

Materials
(for each card)
4 × 5in (10 × 12.5cm) piece of pale green
  Aida fabric, 14 threads to 1in (2.5cm)
Red, white, black and dark grey stranded
  embroidery cottons
Flesh-coloured stranded embroidery
  cotton (for the Santa card)
Silver embroidery thread
Silver, oval-window card blank
All-purpose glue

Working the embroidery
1 Using two strands of embroidery
cotton, work the designs following the
charts, using cross-stitch and three-
quarter cross-stitch. Work the outlines
and mouths in backstitch and use French
knots for the eyes. Work the ermine
lines on Santa's cuffs, coat hem and hat
in black straight stitches. Work silver
double cross-stitches for the stars.

1 sq = 1 cross stitch

92

Finishing

2 Press the embroidery on the wrong side with a warm iron. Trim the fabric edges, mount inside the card, behind the window. Press down firmly with your hand and leave to dry. Glue the return fold around the embroidery.

3 Stick silver thread around the picture ¼in (6mm) from the window edges.

Gift cans

Throw-away food cans can be sprayed with car primer paint and decorated with fibretip pens to make attractive holders for pens, paintbrushes or paper clips.

Materials
Empty cans
Thinners; wire wool
White car primer spray paint
Fibretip pens
Thin card (or stencil blanks)
Masking tape
Sequins (optional)
Scraps of ribbon or braid
All-purpose glue
Latex adhesive

Preparation
1 Wash and remove the label from the can. Clean the out-side surface with thinners and rub down any unevenness with wire wool. Spray inside and outside with several light coats of primer and allow to dry overnight.

2 To make the stencils, trace the shapes and transfer to 2½in (6.5cm) squares of thin card. Using a very sharp craft knife, cut away the shape leaving a clean outline for the stencil. Roll up small pieces of masking tape with the sticky side on the outside, and position around the cut-out design. This will lightly stick the stencil to the can and help you to lift the stencil from the surface of the can smoothly to prevent the ink from running underneath the stencil edges.

Working the design
3 Position the stencil on the can and carefully draw around the inside of the shape with a black fibre-tip pen. Allow to dry, then move the stencil to another position and repeat the process.

4 Add any details freehand (refer to the picture).

5 When the outline is dry, colour in the details. Test the pens on a spare can first. Allow the colours to dry.

6 Add sequins if you like, fixing them in place with a dot of all-purpose glue.

7 Spread latex adhesive around the inside top edge of the can, and then on the back of a piece of ribbon or braid. Leave for a few minutes to become tacky then press the ribbon or braid to the can.

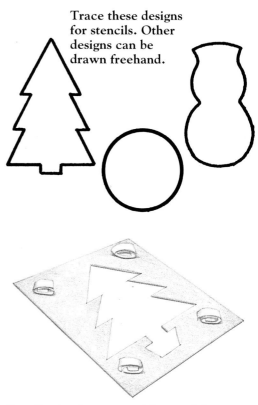

Trace these designs for stencils. Other designs can be drawn freehand.

Fix rolls of sticky tape round the stencil design to help you to lift the stencil.

Better Techniques

***

All kinds of crafts are involved in creating Christmas decorations and gifts. In this chapter you will find useful tips and knowhow for getting a better finish to your projects.

PAPERCRAFTS
Paper and card
Paper and card are used a lot in making Christmas decorations, and of course, for wrapping gifts. There is a wealth to choose from, in a variety of weights, sizes, textures and colours. You will probably be using cartridge or construction paper mostly as this is strong and flexible, folds and creases easily and comes in white only. Cover paper, which is very similar, comes in a good range of shades. Tissue papers are available in wide colour ranges also and good quality tissue is surprisingly strong. Besides providing the perfect finishing touch to gift wrapping you will find it useful for decorating papier mâché items.

Crêpe paper is ideal for a number of decorative crafts, including flower making. Double crêpe paper is obtainable from specialist suppliers and as its name suggests, is of double thickness. Sometimes it is also two-toned and is ideal for creating flower petals.

Another popular craft material is paper ribbon. This is presented wound tightly in coils, so the ribbon has to be gently unfurled to the required width. Although designed for bows and ties it can also be used for plaiting and weaving.

Thin card is sometimes required for making templates. The backs and fronts of cereal packets will do quite well for this.

Giftwrap paper is often underestimated in crafts but you will find its potential is enormous and the design and colour range available seems unlimited. When choosing a giftwrap paper, check that it will fold and crease well without the surface colour flaking and cracking or marking easily. Giftwrap can be laminated to a heavier paper or card for strength and this adds to its versatility. Spray the card or paper with adhesive then 'float' the giftwrap onto it, smoothing the surface from the middle outwards.

Card Artist's mounting card is the thickest card used for crafts projects. It cuts and folds easily and some cards have a coloured backing. Thin card – so thin that it is almost thick paper – is available with a glossy surface. This is ideal for making gift boxes and greeting cards as the surface sheen is an added bonus. If you are unsure of the right card for a project, look at similar designs on sale in the shops, to help guide your choice of thickness.

Special techniques
Scoring
Breaking the surface of card or thick paper with a knife tip to enable a sharper fold to be made.

Laminating
In the context of papercrafts, this involves spraying the surface of card or paper with adhesive, then applying a thinner paper to the surface.

TOOLS AND EQUIPMENT

Most equipment required for craft work is readily available and you may even find you have most of it already. There are a few specialist tools, however, which provide for greater creative possibilities, and help to give crafted items a more professional finish.

The work surface is important. This should be at a good working height, flat and stable. You will require a protective surface to use over the work top, to protect it from cuts and scratches when using craft knives

A sheet of thick card or board is a suitable protection but should be replaced frequently as the surface will become pitted from successive knife cuts. It is worth investing in a special cutting mat. This has a surface which 'heals itself' after every cut and thus remains smooth, and will not distort subsequent cuts made over it.

Cutting tools

You will need two kinds of craft knives: a heavy duty knife, like a Stanley knife or X-acto knife, for cutting thick card, and a small knife, preferably a scalpel, for thin card and paper. Use straight blades, as these suit most tasks, and replace them often for the best results.

You should always cut straight lines by lining the knife up against a firm straight edge. Use a metal rule for this rather than a plastic or wooden ruler, as these materials can easily catch in the blade.

Scissors

You will need several pairs of scissors. For sewing and embroidery projects, you will need dressmaking scissors with sharp blades and pointed tips for cutting out fabric and a small pair of pointed scissors for trimming, snipping and cutting threads.

For non-sewing crafts, have a pair of fairly small, easy-to-handle scissors with straight, pointed blades for most cutting jobs and a longer broad-bladed pair for general cutting. A pair of manicure scissors with curved blades is useful for cutting round intricate shapes.

It is very important that you keep dressmaking scissors quite separate from scissors used for cutting paper. Once scissors have been used to cut paper they will not cut fabric. Tie a piece of brightly coloured thread to the handle of one pair so that you do not mix them up.

Pencils and pens

Pencils are needed for drawing out patterns and for tracing patterns. A dressmakers' chalk pencil is helpful for transferring pattern marks and marking seam lines. Some projects recommend felt-tipped pens and whenever possible, choose waterproof pens.

Measuring aids

A straight-edge ruler is useful for most measuring jobs but if you choose one with a metal edge you can use it for when you are cutting card and paper. You will need a tape measure for sewing crafts. Most tape measures give measurements in both metric and imperial. You will see that the measurements in this book are given in this way, first in imperial (inches and yards) and then in metric (millimetres, centimetres and metres). When you are working a project, use either imperial or metric measurements but do not compare the two because they may not work out exactly the same. Where measurements are critical, an almost exact conversion is given but this is a rare occurrence.

Pattern papers

Two kinds of pattern paper are used in this book. Tracing paper is recommended for tracing same-size patterns but ordinary kitchen greaseproof paper will do just as well. Dressmakers' squared pattern paper, which is available in different scales, is used for enlarging graph patterns. Always check the scale of the pattern before purchasing graph paper.

To use squared pattern paper, you copy the lines of the given graph pattern onto it, square for square.

Needles and pins

For sewing crafts and embroidery you will need a selection of needles. The size for hand-sewing is often a personal preference but generally, medium-sized needles are best for general sewing while short, long-eyed crewel needles are used for embroidery. A long darning needle is useful for working with wool yarn. A bodkin is needed for threading elastic or ribbon through casings or eyelet lace. For embroidery using tapisserie or crewel wool, a tapestry needle is used.

Pins

Glass-headed dressmaker's pins are recommended for craft work because these are easy to see on your work table amongst the other crafts materials (and on the floor) and there is less likelihood of their becoming misplaced. If you are making something that children will hold or play with, count the pins as you use them in the fabric and again when they are removed to make sure that none are left hidden in a seam. Always put pins back in their box or stick them into a pincushion.

Other equipment

In crafts which use paper and card, precise folding and creasing is important. One really useful specialist tool for scoring fold lines on paper is a bookbinder's bone folder, which looks like a small modelling tool. This is drawn against a straight edge and leaves a gentle groove ready for folding. You can improvise, however, by using a knitting needle or a blunt, curve-bladed table knife.

Drawing aids

You will find a protractor useful for drawing diagrams and a pair of pencil compasses is required for drawing circles and arcs. Add a set square to your drawing aids for checking square corners, plus some paper clips and a stapler.

Using geometry equipment
Protractor

This is a half-circle of plastic with degrees marked along the curved edge, from 0° to 180°. In craft work, you need a protractor to assist you in drawing accurate patterns where degrees of angle are given.

To use the protractor, set the straight bottom edge on a straight horizontal line with the vertical, 90° line aligning with any vertical line. Find the desired degree on the edge of the protractor and put a small pencilled mark by it. Remove the protractor and, with a ruler, draw a line from the pencilled mark across to the straight horizontal line where it joins the vertical 90° line. The new line will be at the desired angle from the original line.

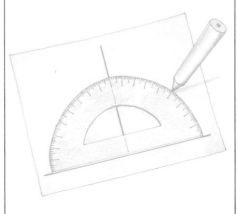

Find the desired degree on the edge of the protractor and put a small pencilled mark by it.

Pair of compasses

These have a steel point at the end of one arm and a pencil is screwed into the other arm. Measure the radius of the desired circle on a ruler using the two arms. Fix the point into the paper lightly and swing the pencil round in a complete circle.

CRAFTS MATERIALS

Adhesives

The types of glue you use are important. Clear, all-purpose glue dries quickly and the long, thin nozzle of the tube makes it easy to apply a tiny dot exactly where it is needed.

Latex adhesive (white from the tube or jar and dries clear) will stick fabrics together and paper to card.

Strong, contact adhesives must be used carefully: they stick fast and very quickly but if you get any on your fingers, you may stick your fingers together! Always follow the manufacturer's instructions to the letter when working with this type of glue.

Glue guns are very useful pieces of equipment if you do a lot of crafts. They are clean and easy to use and the glue, hot when it is applied, dries quickly.

Threads and yarns

It is a basic rule of sewing that the thread should match the fabric not only in colour but in fibre. Use an all-purpose thread when sewing fabrics of man-made fibres. This is a cotton-covered polyester thread that combines strength with good appearance and is suitable for most types of fabric. The colour range is extensive and you can use this thread for most modern fabrics. Soft cotton thread should be used for basting (tacking) and for fabrics made of pure cotton.

Embroidery threads and yarns

When you are working a project is it a good idea to use the thread recommended. Choose a needle to suit the thread. The thread should slip through the eye of the needle easily and the needle should pass through the fabric easily.

Stranded embroidery cotton This comes in a skein and consists of 6 strands loosely twisted together. The strands are used single for very fine work or in combinations.

Pearl cotton This comes in both skeins and balls. It is silky in appearance and comes in three thicknesses.

Soft embroidery cotton This is quite a thick thread and is dull in appearance.

Crewel wool This is a fine, two-ply twisted yarn. For very fine work, the strands can be separated. Crewel wool can be used on both canvas and fabric.

Tapisserie wool Mostly used for canvas work, this comes in a very wide range of colours and is thicker than crewel wool.

Stuffing and filling

Stuffing or toy filling is used quite often in sewing crafts, not only for toys but also for sachets, pincushions etc. A poor, lumpy filling can spoil even the most exquisitely made piece so it is worth investing in the best stuffing you can afford. Polyester toy filling, which is flameproof, is undoubtedly the best. It washes well, dries quickly, is lightweight and very resilient – and it has the added advantage that it is white and does not show through light-coloured fabrics.

Paints

Paints used in crafts include poster paints, acrylics, water colours and designer gouache. If they are recommended, you can also use household emulsion paint, model makers' enamel paints, as well as multi-purpose metallic paint.

Varnish

Varnish for finishing and protecting work can be gloss, satin or matt finish. A spray fixative can be used to protect the surface of finished work, making it less likely to mark or stain.

Stuffing tool

If you are doing a lot of toymaking, it is a good idea to make yourself a special stuffing tool. Take a short length of $\frac{1}{4}$in (6mm) diameter wood dowelling – about 12in (30cm) will be sufficient. Shape one end to a blunt point, using first a craft knife then sandpaper. Sandpaper the point until it is smooth.

Useful and decorative stitches
Here are some stitches you will use in this book.

Basting or tacking Small even stitches worked along the seam line to hold two layers of fabric together for stitching.

Gathering Small, even stitches worked across the fabric and then pulled up to form gathers.

Gathering

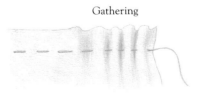

Oversewing Neat stitches worked over the edges of fabric to neaten them or to close an open seam (A – B – C).

Oversewing

Slip stitch is used for closing a seam and is almost invisible if properly worked.

Slip stitch

Back stitch can be used instead of machine-stitching seaming (A – B – C).

Back stitch

Satin stitch consists of straight stitches worked side by side and touching and is used for filling shapes (A – B – C).

Satin stitch

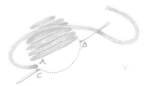

Stem stitch is a linear stitch and is often used for working stems. In toy making, it is often recommended for working eyebrows and mouths (A – B – C).

Stem stitch

Cross stitch is worked on evenweave fabric. In the first stage, diagonal stitches are worked from right to left across a certain number of fabric threads. In the second stage diagonal stitches are worked from left to right to complete the cross stitch.

Cross stitch

Half cross stitch is often used in canvas work. Only the first stage of diagonal stitches is used.

Half cross stitch

Three-quarter cross stitch This is used in some cross stitch projects to give a more rounded edge to a shape. The first half of the cross is formed in the usual way then the 'quarter' stitch is brought across and down into the central hole.

Three-quarter cross stitch

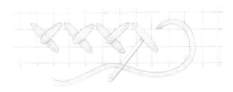

SEWING CRAFTS TECHNIQUES
Working with plastic canvas
Plastic canvas is useful for making embroidered items where rigidity is required – such as tree ornaments, boxes, doll's house furniture, planters, tissue box toppers, waste baskets and desk accessories – and much, much more. There is no trick to using it. Any stitches which can be used on woven canvas can be used on the plastic kind.

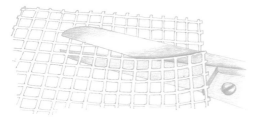

Cut out plastic canvas leaving a solid edge.

Understanding patterns
Pattern instructions will either tell you to cut canvas to measurements or to a given number of holes (not threads). If you are working with a given size, you work the design from the chart then trim the excess canvas away afterwards. If you are working to holes, it is a good idea to first trace out the shape you are working, on the canvas, using a grease or wax pencil. Whichever method you use make quite sure you have allowed enough holes for the design before cutting out and that the edges of the canvas are solid plastic and not ends of 'threads'. The edges must be solid because you are going to neaten them overcasting.

Special tip
If certain edges of the shape you are working need rounding off, trim away the very tip of the plastic at the corners (taking care not to cut through the plastic 'thread'). This also helps the corner overcasting to lie more smoothly.

Creativity with plastic canvas
Almost any kind of thread or yarn can be used on plastic canvas, as long as the thread will pass through the holes and covers the plastic adequately. Fine threads, such as stranded embroidery cotton, can be doubled up to 12 strands or used to overwork wool embroidery. Metallic threads and beads add glitter – ideal if you are working Christmas decos.

Yarns
Acrylic yarns are ideal for working on plastic canvas but any yarn, such as 'worsted-weight' will do, as long as it is thick enough to cover the canvas.

Starting and finishing
Take the needle through from the right side, leaving a 'tail' and bring the needle up in the place you intend to start stitching. When a few stitches have been worked, take the tail through to the wrong side and thread it through the back of the worked stitches. When finishing, thread the yarn end through the back of stitches in the same way.

Neatening the edges
Overcasting is used to neaten the edges of the finished embroidery. Use a matching yarn colour unless otherwise instructed. It may be necessary to go through a hole more than once to get an even coverage on the edge, especially at the corners.

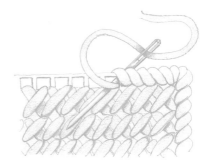

Work oversewing over the edges to finish.

102

RIBBONS AND BOWS

You will probably be using three kinds of ribbon for your decorations and giftwrapping. The water-resistant type which florists use (sometimes called 'cut-edge' because it is cut from rolls of fabric) is ideal for both tying and wiring bows. Gift tie ribbon, sold on spools, sticks to itself when moistened and is perfect for making all kinds of bows and rosettes. Paper ribbon comes in a tightly twisted rope and, when unfurled, makes big, flamboyant bows. You may also be able to find a special ribbon in the shops which has a fine wire in the edges. This enables you to bend bows and streamers into shape.

Wired bow

Using florists' ribbon or gift tie ribbon, form a length into a figure-of-eight. With the same length, make another figure-of-eight, holding the bows together. Bind the two bows together with wire, leaving two 'legs'.

Sew the ribbon together across the width. Cut the ends off diagonally.

Fold a short piece of ribbon, wrap it round the bow's waist.

Make two figure-of-eights with ribbon.

Wire together, leaving two wire legs.

Sew the ribbon ends together on the back of the bow.

Paper ribbon bows

Untwist 3yd (2.75m) of ribbon rope. Make a small 2in (5cm) loop and bind with wire. Make a second loop, slightly larger and bind again. Continue, making loops of increasing size, binding each tightly in the same position. Twist the wire ends together, leaving two legs.

Tailored bow

You can make this with gift tie or woven acetate ribbons. Either sew or stick the bow together. Cut ribbon to the desired length, fold in half and sew across the width, slightly less than halfway from the ends. Cut the ends diagonally. Bring the sewn seam to the middle and baste together. Press. Cut another, small piece of ribbon. Fold the edges under. Fold the ribbon over the middle of the bow, overlapping at the back. Sew the edges together on the back.

GREETING CARDS

The custom of sending greeting cards at Christmas was started by the Victorians in the late 19th century. At first, cards were simply pretty, with flowers and love messages. Later, as colour printing became cheaper, cards became elaborate with tinsel and gold paper lace, angels and cherubims, holly and robins, richly decked trees and rosy-cheeked, angelic children. However, the Victorians also loved hand-made cards and were clever and innovative in their creation. Hand-made cards are appreciated and treasured just as much today.

For all hand-made cards, use good quality art paper or thin, white card. Buy the envelopes first and make the cards about ¼in (6mm) smaller all round so that they fit into the envelopes. For bulky designs (such as dried flower collage) make shallow boxes from stiff card and pack the corners with polystyrene packing to prevent the flowers from getting squashed in the post.

Measure and pencil out the card, ensuring the corners are square with a set square. Use a sharp scalpel to cut out, cutting against the edge of a metal ruler. Score along the fold line on the outside.

Window cards

These can either have a single fold or two folds. To make a two-fold card, cut card to three times the width of the finished card. Measure and score two folds. Draw and cut a window in the centre section. The decoration is positioned behind the window and the left-hand section folded over and stuck down.

Windows can also be cut to seasonal shapes, bells, trees, stars etc.

Ideas for cards
Victorian-style

Choose a pastel colour for the basic card. Select a suitable picture from an old Christmas card or buy reproduction Victorian motifs. Cut the picture to an oval or circular shape. Trace round the picture on the card. Stick narrow, pre-gathered lace round the marked line. Stick the picture over the lace. Add a small ribbon bow. Alternatively, edge the picture with gold or silver paper doyley.

Another effect is achieved by sticking a round picture to the middle of a small paper doyley and then mounting the doyley on a card.

Simple cut-outs

Trace simple festive shapes – bells, candles, a snowman, a tree, holly sprig etc. Transfer to thin card and cut out a template. Use the template to cut shapes from coloured or metallic paper. Stick the shapes to the fronts of cards. Add glitter pen decoration, sequins, beads etc. For instance, add a red ribbon bow to two gold-paper bells. Or cut candle flames from gold paper, stick over coloured paper candle shapes, add thin lines of gold glitter paint. For a Christmas tree, cut a green paper triangle, add sequins for baubles and tiny, strung beads for garlands.

Embroidered cards

Cross stitch, canvas embroidery, free-style embroidery and appliqué can all be used for window greeting cards. Work the embroidery, trim the fabric to a size

Cut the window in the centre section of the card. The left-hand section folds back over the window.

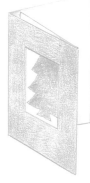

slightly smaller than the card and stick behind the window of a two-fold card.

Alternatively, stick coloured or plain acetate behind the window and then stick strips of paper over the acetate to represent window panes. A picture can be stuck onto the third section so that it is viewed through the window.

3-D decoupage cards

Cut and fold a single fold card. Laminate a sheet of giftwrap to thin card, using spray adhesive. Cut out 4 identical motifs. Trace round one motif on the greeting card. Cut double-sided adhesive pads into small pieces. Stick bits down all over the motif area. Peel off the paper backing. Stick another cut-out motif on top, exactly matching the edges. Decide which areas of the motif you want to lift forward, bearing in mind that the foreground detail should be the top layer of your design. Place sticky pads on your selected areas. Cut out the relevant details from the third motif. Continue, adding sticky pads to the chosen areas and cut details from the fourth motif.

Flower collage cards

This technique can be used for greeting cards all year round. Press flowers and leaves in the summer and store them in acetate envelopes. Arrange the dried, pressed material on a sheet of paper. Stick pieces down, overlapping some in a natural way, using touches of clear, all-purpose adhesive, applied with a toothpick. Leave to dry. (It is better not to use latex adhesive because the adhesive can soak into the petals and cannot be removed.) Peel the backing from a sheet of transparent adhesive film. Gently lift onto the flower collage and smooth out from the centre. Press around the edges of the collage with a finger tip to exclude any air bubbles. Trim the paper to size and stick behind the opening of a window card.

Abstract designs

Choose a colour picture from a magazine that has suitably 'festive' colours. Have it enlarged on a colour photostat machine in 'contour mode'. The detail will disappear and a fascinating, abstract effect is achieved. Cut the photostat into shapes and stick onto prepared cards.

Cover the whole motif with sticky pads. Then put the second motif on top.

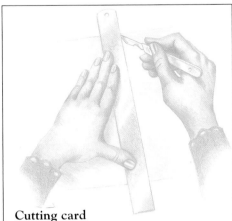

Cutting card

Align the ruler against the line to be cut. Firmly draw the knife towards you and score the line gently. Then, without moving the ruler, cut again to cut through the card.

FLOWER CRAFTS

Pressed flowers

The secret of successful flower pressing is patience. Once you have put it away the plant material should be left for at least four weeks. You can, of course, leave flowers and leaves for longer. The more time you give the process the better the final result will be. The material will be paper thin and the colours are less likely to fade when you use it for cards or pictures.

Most flowers will press well. Bell-shaped flowers such as snowdrops, lily-of-the-valley, Canterbury bells and daffodils should be sliced in half. Large flowers with fleshy centres can have their petals pressed separately. Flowers with large heads – such as hydrangea – can be separated into individual florets. For greeting cards, press some leaves as well. Ivy leaves retain their colour and small fern fronds look pleasing with flower arrangements. Silvery-toned leaves, such as silver carpet, look like little snow-covered trees when dried.

Lay the flowers and leaves on the blotting paper.

Flower press

Flower presses can be purchased from crafts suppliers but you can press flowers almost as well in a large book. Choose one with a large page size and a lot of pages. Start at the back. Spread a sheet of white blotting paper on the page. Lay the flowers on the paper (they should not touch or overlap) then place another sheet of blotting paper on top. Turn several pages of the book then insert another sheet of blotting paper and arrange the next group of flowers. Continue until the book is full. It is a good idea to keep a note of what is on each page. Leave the book, undisturbed, with a weight on top for at least four weeks, longer if possible.

Preserved flowers

Pick flowers and grasses for preserving on a dry day as soon as the dew has dried off and the sap is rising.

Air and water drying

Upside-down method Fix a pole or line across an airy, dark room. Strip the foliage from the flowers. Arrange bunches with their heads at different levels and secure the stems with a rubber band. Bend 'S' hooks from strong wire and use these to hang the bunches from the line or pole. Do not have too many flowers in a bunch and leave space between the hanging bunches. Leave the flowers until they feel papery and dry.

Standing method Grasses, Chinese lanterns, sea lavender, statice and bulrushes are best dried upright in a container of dry sand.

Water drying This is a good method for hydrangea heads. Pick the flowers and place the stems in a container with 1in (2.5cm) of water. Allow to dry out and do not replenish the water.

Hang bunches, heads down, on 'S' hooks.

Dessicant drying

The most commonly used dessicants are borax, crushed silica gel and silver sand. Detergent powder can also be used.

You need a large tin or plastic box with an airtight lid. Place a layer of the dessicant in the base of the box. Cut the flower stems to ½in (1cm), sufficient to attach a wire after drying. Carefully lay the flowers in the dessicant, making sure they do not touch. Using a spoon, slowly trickle dessicant amongst the petals and continue doing this until they are covered to a depth of about 1in (2.5cm). Seal on the lid.

Trickle dessicant between the petals.

Inspect the flowers after a few days. They are ready when they are dry and feel papery. With silica gel, the process may take only 2–4 days.

Carefully pour off the dessicant into another container and pick out the flowers, one at a time, as they come to the surface. Lay them on a plate or tray and carefully brush any remaining dessicant from the petals with an artist's soft paint brush.

Turn the flowers upside-down on soft, folded muslin and stick on false wire stems, using clear, all-purpose adhesive. Cover the wire with stem tape.

Preserving foliage

Although leaves can be preserved by

Stand the branches in a jar of glycerine solution.

pressing, a glycerine solution is mostly used to preserve whole branches of leaves. Glycerine will change the colours of leaves to shades of brown but they retain their suppleness.

Make up a mixture of 60% glycerine to 40% hot water. Mix and pour the liquid into a glass jar and put the jar into a large container (such as a bucket or pail). Strip the lower foliage from the branches and scrape the bark from the bottom 2in (5cm) of the stems. Crush the ends with a hammer and put the stems into the jar so that the bucket or pail supports the branches.

Depending on the type of foliage, it will take between 1 and 4 weeks for the leaves to be preserved.

Stick a wire stem onto the flower with clear adhesive.

Cover the wire stem with stem tape.

CHRISTMAS CRACKERS

Christmas crackers originated with the Christmas-loving Victorians. They are still an important part of Christmas festivities, especially for children. Lavishly trimmed and with a little gift hidden inside, crackers make an important contribution to the decoration of the party table, adding colour and sparkle – and the element of surprise!. Although most people buy their own, crackers are very easy to make. Complete cracker-making kits are sometimes to be found around Christmas in crafts shops and have the added advantage that you can choose the gifts that go inside.

Decorating crackers

If you are making your own crackers, you can let your imagination run free with the decorating of them. For instance, for decorative banding, cut strips of foil paper with pinking shears and stick round the cracker about 1in (2.5cm) from each end.

Or make frills from crêpe paper. Cut a strip for each end 6 × 8in (15 × 20cm), with the grain running crossways. Cut a scalloped edge on one side. Run gathering stitches across the length, about 2½in (6cm) from the edge. Pull up the gathers and fold on the gathering. Brush clear glue on the scalloped edges and dip in glitter dust. Tie the frills round the waists of the cracker.

Choose decorations to fit in with your table scheme. For example, make tiny bunches of dried flowers to match your centrepiece, or wire small fir cones or poppy seed heads together and spray them gold or silver. Dip them in glitter dust before the paint dries. Tie decorations to the crackers with very narrow ribbons.

CARNIVAL HATS

Inexpensive and colourful party hats can be made from crêpe paper and thin cardboard. Keep the shapes simple – crowns, cones, caps, pill boxes etc and decorate for different effects.

Crown

Measure round the head. Cut crêpe paper to this measurement plus 1in (2.5cm) for overlap by 5in (12.5cm). Cut one long edge into points or scallops. Cut circles, squares and diamond shapes from foil paper. Stick along the crown. Overlap and stick the ends.

Cone

Cut an 18in (45cm) radius half-circle of thin card. Cut the same shape in crêpe paper. Fasten together on the edges with double-sided tape. Form the paper-covered card into a cone. Tape the overlap to fit the head. Trim the bottom edge if necessary. Decorate with paper pompons, fringing or foil stars.

Pill box

Cut a strip of thin card to fit round the head plus 1in (2.5cm) overlap by 6in (15cm). Cut a piece of crêpe paper to the same length by 8in (20cm). Form the card into a ring and tape or stick the overlap. Do the same with the crêpe paper. Gather one end of the crêpe paper ring. Pull up the gathers tightly. Trim the paper close to the stitching. Slip the paper ring over the card ring. Pull the excess paper to the bottom of the ring, tuck inside and tape to the inside edge. Cut a circle of foil paper and stick it over the gathered top.

Cap

Make a pill box from card and paper. Cut a brim from card and tape to the bottom edge.

Witch's hat

Make a cone from card and black crêpe paper. Cut a circle of black card and cut out the middle to fit the bottom of the cone. Tape together.

Flower circlet

Make several tissue paper or crêpe paper pompons. Cut a piece of 1in (2.5cm)-wide ribbon to tie round the head with long streamers hanging down. Cut the ends diagonally. Starting in the middle of the circlet, sew on the paper pompons, close together.

MASKS

Make these from felt. Iron lightweight interfacing onto one side. Draw the pattern on squared pattern paper. Pin to the felt and cut out. Cut out the eye holes. Cut a head band from shirring elastic and sew the ends to either side of the mask. If you prefer, sew on pieces of narrow ribbon and tie the mask on at the back of the head.

Decorating masks

● Stick lengths of sequins or tiny beads round the mask and round the eye holes.
● Cut a fringe from felt and stick along the bottom edge of the mask.
● Paint scrolls, lines and spots with a glitter pen.
● Make the mask in black felt, paint white whiskers from each side of the nose. Paint a white line round the eyes.
● Make the mask in red felt but cut the eyes at a greater slant. Paint long black eyelashes round the eyes.

Scale: 1 sq = ½in (1cm)

WOODCRAFT TOOLS

For simple toymaking you need only basic woodworking tools.

Crafts knife This is useful for cutting shapes from soft wood – such as balsa wood.

Gents saw (small hacksaw) This is ideal for small-scale work in both softwoods and hard woods. Various sizes are available, from about 4in (10cm) long.

Fretsaw (jigsaw) This has a very fine blade fitted into a u-shaped handle.

Hand drill for drilling holes. An electric drill is quicker but not essential.

Hammer A small hammer is more useful than a big one.

Surform tools These are available in a variety of shapes and sizes and can be used for shaping wood, plastic and some metals. The blades are pierced (like a cheese grater) and are replaceable.

Files These also come in a wide range of shapes and sizes, flat, half-rounded and round. The words 'bastard files' is a term for a range of files, used by woodworkers for generations.

Screwdriver For toymaking, one or two hand screwdrivers are sufficient.

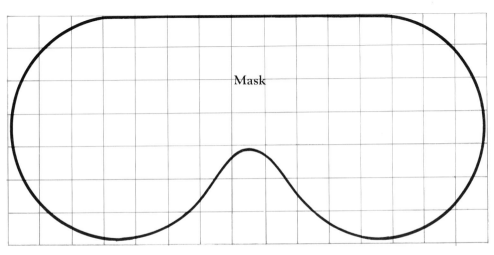

Mask

CANDLEMAKING

The winter holiday is a festival of light in many parts of the world and candles are an important part of both religious and secular celebrations. There are many ways of decorating bought candles to give them a special festive look but you may like to try making your own candles at home.

Special kits are available, containing everything you need but the basic materials can also be purchased separately from candle makers' suppliers.

A simple, one-colour candle should be your first project. You can go on to more exciting designs and forms later.

You will need a double boiler for melting the wax and stearin, a sugar thermometer, a dye disc to colour the candle, a wick, a candle mould and a container of cold water.

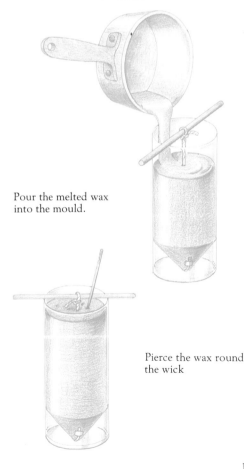

Pour the melted wax into the mould.

Pierce the wax round the wick

To begin, put 1 tablespoon (25gms) of stearin into the top of the double boiler. Melt over a low heat. When the stearin has melted, add about ⅛th of the dye disc and allow to dissolve.

Now add 11 tablespoons (225 gms) of paraffin wax granules and heat gently to 180°F (82°C).

Dip the wick in the wax to prime it and allow to set. Thread the wick through the hole in the base of the mould. Tie a thin stick or a large needle to the other end of the wick. Pull the wick through the base of the mould to tighten it so that the stick rests across the top of the mould. Seal the hole around the wick at the other end with a lump of mould seal (or plasticine) to make sure the mould is leakproof.

Check that the wax is still at 180°F (82°C) and pour carefully into the mould. Leave it for a minute then give the mould a sharp tap to release any air bubbles.

Stand the mould in a bowl of cold water with a weight on top.

After a while, a well will form round the wick. Lift the mould out of the water and pierce the wax round the wick. Top up with wax heated to 200°F (93°F). Replace the mould in the cold water. Leave the candle until it is set.

Remove the mould seal and slip the candle out of the mould. Trim the wick at the base. If the base seems uneven, heat an old saucepan and smooth the candle off by moving it around on the bottom of the saucepan.

Wired candles

To ensure that candles can be lifted from candleholders easily, wire the ends. Cut 3in (7.5cm) lengths of stem wires and hold them round the candle end, with the ends protruding underneath. Bend the ends under the candle and bind them all together with wire. Insert into the candleholder.

FESTIVE CANDLE HOLDERS
Fringed
Cover a small jar with 3 layers of pasted newspaper pieces. Leave to dry. Coat with white emulsion paint. Cut a piece of thick, cotton fringe to fit round the jar. Dip it into PVA adhesive cover it and fit the fringe round the jar. Spread the fringe ends and leave to dry. Paint the fringe with acrylic colours if you like.

Slip pieces of card between the containers.

Spread the fringe ends and leave to dry.

Classic shape
Collect a group of containers – jars, plastic pots with lids, small cans, cottage cheese tubs etc. Cut pieces of thick card to squares, circles, hexagons and pentagons. Arrange one container on another, the largest at the bottom and slipping pieces of card in between. Stick or tape the structure together. Cover with pasted strips of newspaper. Apply 6–7 layers. When the candle holder is dry, coat with 2 layers of white emulsion paint. To decorate, paint in a single colour (gold looks effective). Add black or white painted designs. Alternatively, stick pieces of string or braid round the candle holder, then paint with acrylic paint. Finish the candle holder with a coat of clear varnish.

PAPERCRAFTS GLOSSARY
Canson paper
This is a textured art paper and comes in about 20 shades.

Cartridge paper or construction paper
This comes in different weights and qualities in white only. *Cover paper* which is similar in weight comes in several colours.

Ingres paper
This is a thin art paper with a texture of thin lines. It is available in a good colour range.

Corrugated card (railroad card)
This is available in two forms. In one, the corrugated surface is open to one side. In the other, the corrugations are enclosed between two smooth surfaces.

Brown paper (Kraft paper)
Ordinary brown, good quality parcel wrapping paper.

Mounting card (mount card)
Available in 3 qualities, 4, 6 and 8 sheet, 4 being the thinnest. It is available in a range of colours, including black and grey, all with a white back.

Useful addresses

Candlemakers Supplies Ltd
28 Blythe Road, London, W14 0HA
Tel: 071 602 4031
Candlemaking equipment and kits
(Will supply by post)

Fred Aldous Ltd
37 Lever Street, Manchester 1, M60 1UX
Tel: 061 236 2477
Most craft materials including craft foil,
   cotton balls, crêpe paper, felt etc.
(Will supply by post. Send for catalogue)

C M Offray & Son Ltd
Fir Tree Place, Church Road, Ashford,
   Middlesex, TW15 2PH
Tel: 0784 247281
Woven satin and gift ribbons
(Write for address of nearest stockist)

Rose & Hubble Ltd
2/4 Relay Road, White City, London,
   W12 7SJ
Tel: 081 749 8822
Fabric including Christmas print fabrics

Appleton Brothers Ltd,
Thames Works, Church Street,
Chiswick, London, W4
Crewel wool

Acknowledgements

The author and publishers would like to
thank the following companies and
individuals who assisted in the
preparation of this book:

Appleton Brothers Ltd for crewel wools

Coats Patons Crafts for stranded
   embroidery threads

Candlemakers Supplies Ltd for the
   appliqué candle

Fred Aldous Ltd for craft materials

C M Offray & Son Ltd for ribbons

Rose & Hubble Ltd for Christmas
   fabrics

Heather Best of Best Floral Designs,
Yeovil, who designed and made the Rope
of flowers on page 18, the Flower cones
on page 23, and the Table arrangement
on pages 68–69.

The Christmas Shop, Hays Galleria,
Tooley Street, London SE1 2HD for
supplying artificial Christmas trees.

Julia Harvey, for all her help with the
typing of the manuscript.